RECOVERY DHARMA

RECOVERY DHARMA

*How to use Buddhist practices and principles
to heal the suffering of addiction*

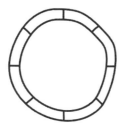

second edition

RECOVERY DHARMA GLOBAL

recoverydharma.org

recovery dharma *global*

We dedicate this book to the South Asian and Asian ancestors who protected and freely offered the Buddha's teachings to all. Buddhism originated in India and later flourished in other regions of Asia, including South Asia, East Asia, Southeast Asia, Central Asia, and others.

We express deep gratitude to the cultural heritage that our program is founded on. We recognize and appreciate that many of our meetings are held on ancestral indigenous ground that were never ceded. We honor those who have committed to the ongoing stewardship of this land.

Likewise, we honor the communities of Black, Indigenous, and people of color, recognizing the systemic oppression and marginalization that members of these communities may have experienced in the world and in recovery spaces.

We dedicate our practice to fostering collective healing and liberation from all oppressions, the tormenting cycle of addiction, and suffering, as one human race. We wholeheartedly embrace all those who wish to pursue recovery as part of our community, regardless of race, ethnicity, gender, sexual orientation, age, disability, or nationality.

With all of the joy and sadness, skillfulness and imperfection, striving and resting, grasping and letting go that arise on this path of healing and growth, we honor all those who have walked the grateful road of recovery in the past, present, and those who will carry on this practice in the future.

∞

CONTENTS

Appendix:

PREFACE

Once we make a decision to recover from addiction — to substances, habits, people, whatever — it can be scary. The feeling is often one of loss and loneliness, because recovery can shake our sense of some of our core identities, and the concept of who we are. How will I relate to others? How can I remain steadfast in my decision? Change can be hard to face, even if we know we're letting go of something that's a danger to us. Recovery Dharma offers resources and a supportive setting for this brave change no matter what part of the journey you're on.

This book presents the use of Buddhist practices and principles to recover from addiction of all kinds, without the requirement of becoming a Buddhist. The Buddha taught that due to craving, greed, anger, and confusion, the mind may be a source of great suffering. With this path, we're using an ancient and proven way to transform our minds and behavior. We're choosing to trust in our own potential for wisdom, awakening, and compassion for others and ourselves.

This book is a collaboration from members of our community. It's intended as a supportive guide for those new to this path as well as long-term practitioners. It's structured around the "three jewels" of Buddhism: the **Buddha** (the potential for our own awakening and the goal of the path), the **Dharma** (the teachings/how we get there), and the **Sangha** (our community of wise friends/who we travel with). We'll share how we have used these teachings to recover from addiction in a way that honors what is wise and helpful for us individually, as opposed to a one-size-fits-all approach.

Each of us has our own unique identities and life experiences. Some of us have experienced trauma or lifelong challenges due to being a minority in race, ethnicity, gender, sexual orientation, social class status, disability status, etc. Our program recognizes that being in recovery also means healing and gaining wisdom within our own social identities. We encourage you to adapt this book and create inquiries that may help promote healing, growth, and understanding based on your own identity and experience.

WHAT IS RECOVERY DHARMA?

Dharma is a Sanskrit word meaning "truth," "phenomena," or "the nature of things." When it's capitalized, Dharma usually means the teachings of the Buddha and the practices based on those teachings.

The Buddha knew that all human beings, to some extent, struggle with craving — the powerful, sometimes blinding desire to change our thoughts, feelings, or circumstances. Those of us who experience addiction have been driven to use substances and/or harmful behaviors in a habitual pattern to try and create this desired change. Even though the Buddha didn't talk specifically about addiction, he understood the obsessive nature of the human mind. He understood our attachment to pleasure and aversion to pain. He understood the extreme measures we are willing to take, chasing what we want to feel and running away from feelings we fear. And he found a solution.

This book describes a way to free ourselves from the suffering of addiction using Buddhist practices and principles. This program leads to recovery from addiction to substances like alcohol and drugs and from *process addictions* like sex, gambling, pornography, technology, work, codependence, shopping, eating, media, self-harm, lying, stealing, and obsessive worrying. This is a path to freedom from any repetitive and habitual behavior that causes suffering.

Some of us reading this book may be unfamiliar with Buddhism or have not used Buddhist practices as a pathway to recovery. There might also be unfamiliar Buddhist words and concepts in this book. We also understand that what we present in this book does not encompass all Buddhist traditions, lineages, teachings, and practices, and may to some extent differ from your own Buddhist practice. Our aim is to clearly describe our path and practice in Recovery Dharma for people new to recovery, new to Buddhism, and for those familiar with both. This book describes the original Buddhist teachings from which our program comes, the essence of Buddhism's fundamental and early teachings — the Four Noble Truths — to show how practicing the Eightfold Path is a pragmatic pathway which can transform the challenges of both early and long-term recovery.

This is a renunciation-based program. Regardless of our individual addictions, all of our members commit to a basic abstinence from that substance or behavior. For process addictions like food and technology, renunciation may mean establishing thoughtful boundaries and intentions. For some of us, abstinence from things like obsessive sexual behavior, or compulsively seeking out love and relationships, may be necessary as we work to understand and find meaningful boundaries. Many of us have found that after renouncing our primary addiction for a period of time, other harmful behaviors and process addictions become apparent in our lives. Rather than getting discouraged, we found that we can meet these behaviors with compassion, wisdom, and patient investigation into our habitual tendencies. We believe recovery is a lifelong, holistic process of peeling back layers of habits and conditioned behaviors to find our own potential for awakening.

Our program is peer-led: we do not follow any one teacher or leader. We support each other as partners walking the path of recovery together. This is not a program based in dogma or religion, but in finding the truth for ourselves. This insight has worked for us, but is not the only path. It's fully compatible with other spiritual paths and programs of recovery. We know from our own experience that true recovery is only possible with the intention of radical honesty, understanding, awareness, and integrity, and we trust you to discover your own path.

This is a program that asks us to never stop growing. It asks us to own our choices and be responsible for our own healing. It's based on mindfulness, kindness, generosity, forgiveness, and deep compassion.

We do not rely on methods of shame and fear as motivators. These haven't worked in our own pasts, and have often created more struggle and suffering through relapse and discouragement. The courage it takes to recover from addiction is ultimately courage of the heart, and we aim to support each other as we commit to this brave work.

Many of us have spent a lot of time criticizing ourselves. In this program, we renounce violence and doing harm, including the violence and harm we do to ourselves. We believe in the healing power of forgiveness. We put our trust in our own potential to awaken and recover, in the Four Noble Truths of the Buddha, and in the people we meet and connect with in meetings and throughout our journey in recovery.

Of course we cannot escape the circumstances and conditions that are part of the human condition. We've already tried — through drugs and alcohol, through sex and codependency, through gambling and technology, through work and shopping, through food or the restriction of food, through obsession and the futile attempts to control our experiences and feelings — and we're here because it didn't work. This is a program that invites us to recognize and accept that some pain and disappointment will always be present, to investigate the unskillful ways we have dealt with that pain in the past, and to develop a habit of understanding, compassion, forgiveness, and insight toward our own pain, the pain of others, and the pain we have caused. Acceptance with insight and compassion is what creates freedom from the suffering that makes our pain seem unbearable.

This book is only an introduction to a path that can bring liberation and freedom from the cycle of addiction. The intention, and the hope of our program, is that every person on the path will be empowered to make it their own.

> May you be happy.
> May you be at ease.
> May you be free from suffering.
> May all beings be free from suffering.

WHERE TO BEGIN

How *can* we use Buddhism for our recovery? Outlined below are the areas that we suggest you concentrate your energy on while walking this path.

We come to understand the Four Noble Truths and use them as a guide for our path of recovery. This program doesn't ask us to believe in anything other than our own potential to wake up: just allowing ourselves to believe that it's possible, or even *might* be possible. Through experiential learning, we realize that our efforts can make a difference and this is a way to recover. Then we make a decision to repeatedly commit to this path.

As we learn about the Four Noble Truths — including the Eightfold Path that leads to the end of the suffering caused by addiction — we put these principles into practice in our lives. This book presents an introduction to these Truths and the Eightfold Path as a guide to a non-harming way of being in the world. It is both a philosophy and a plan of action.

Meditation is an essential part of the program. This book contains some basic instructions for you so you can start right away. Most of us have found it very helpful to attend meetings that include an opportunity to practice meditation with others. A key to this program is establishing a regular meditation practice — in and outside of meetings. This will help us begin the process of investigating our own minds, our reactivity, and our behavior. We look deeply at the nature and causes of our suffering so we can find a path to freedom that's based on authentic self-knowledge.

The subsequent chapters discuss three aspects of the program — the "three jewels" of Buddhism: the Buddha, the Dharma, and the Sangha — as a way of developing the wisdom, ethical conduct, and spiritual practice that leads to recovery. We hope that groups and individuals will use this book to customize their own course of recovery. We offer some suggestions in that spirit. You're invited to take what works for you and leave the rest.

At the end of each section are inquiries for self-exploration. These questions can be used as part of a formal process with a mentor, wise friend, or group; as tools to explore a specific life situation; as guides for a daily self-inquiry practice; or as meeting discussion topics. A wise friend or mentor can be of great help in deepening your understanding, and we encourage you to reach out to people you encounter at meetings.

Supportive friendships are an integral part of the practice. The questions may bring up shame, guilt, or sadness; or they may possibly activate trauma. It could be beneficial to set up a self-care strategy ahead of time. The intent of the questions is to deepen our practice so we can experience more freedom, not to bring us more suffering.

Our path is not a checklist, but rather a practice in which we choose where and how to invest our energy in a way that is both wise and compassionate toward ourselves and others. This journey involves meditation, meetings, and written inventories, all of which can improve our lives greatly. The practice of the Eightfold Path helps us develop insight and compassion as we begin to look into the causes and conditions that led to our own suffering with addiction. This path doesn't have an end. There will continue to be suffering and challenges in life. This path offers a way to transform the suffering caused by our habitual reactions to these challenges, and an end to the illusion of escape we tried to find in substances or behaviors. It's a way to break our chains with our own hands. It's a path of deep freedom and refuge.

THE PRACTICE

Renunciation: We understand addiction to describe the overwhelming craving and compulsive use of substances or behaviors to escape present-time reality, either by clinging to pleasure or running from pain. We commit to the intention of abstinence from alcohol and other addictive substances. For those of us recovering from process addictions, particularly those for which complete abstinence is not possible, we also identify and commit to wise boundaries around our harmful behaviors, preferably with the help of a mentor or therapeutic professional.

Meditation: We commit to the intention of developing a daily meditation practice. We use meditation as a tool to investigate our actions, intentions, reactivity, and the nature of our mind. Meditation is a personal practice, and we commit to finding a balanced effort toward this and other healthy practices on the path.

Meetings: We attend recovery meetings whenever possible, in person and/or online, whether it be with Recovery Dharma, other Buddhist communities, or other recovery fellowships. In early recovery, it is recommended to attend a recovery meeting as often as possible. We also commit to becoming an active part of the community, offering our own experiences and service wherever possible.

The Path: We commit to deepening and broadening our understanding of the Four Noble Truths and to practicing the Eightfold Path in our daily lives.

Inquiry and Investigation: We explore the Four Noble Truths through writing and sharing in-depth, detailed inquiries. These can be worked on with the guidance of a mentor or therapist, in partnership with a trusted friend, or with a group. As we complete our written inquiries, we strive to hold ourselves accountable and take direct responsibility for our actions using wise intentions. This includes making amends for the harm we have caused in our past.

Sangha, Wise Friends, Mentors: We cultivate relationships within a recovery community, to support our own recovery and the recovery of others. After we have completed significant work on our inquiries, established a meditation practice, and achieved renunciation from our addictive behaviors, we can become mentors to help others on their path to liberation from addiction. Anyone with any period of time of renunciation and practice can be of service to others in their sangha. When mentors are not available, a group of wise friends can act as partners in self-inquiry and support each other's practice.

Growth: We continue our study of Buddhist practices through reading, listening to Dharma talks, visiting and becoming members of recovery and spiritual sanghas, and attending meditation or retreats to enhance our understanding, wisdom, and practice. We undertake a lifelong journey of growth and awakening.

I.

AWAKENING: BUDDHA

Most of us enter recovery with one goal in mind: to stop the suffering that got us here in the first place, whether that was drinking, using drugs, stealing, eating, gambling, sex, codependency, technology, or other process addictions. As newcomers, most of us would be satisfied with simple damage control or reduction in harmful behavior. We want to stop hurting ourselves or others in particular ways.

You're reading this because there is a spark of wisdom in you that desires to seek the end of the suffering of your addiction. You've already taken the first step on the path to your own awakening. Everyone who has made the wise intention to recover, wherever they are on their path, has accessed that pure, wise part of themselves that the wreckage of addiction can never touch.

So many of us have hearts that are still in pain from the suffering we've experienced. Some have undergone trauma which often led us to seek temporary relief in our addictive behavior which unintentionally added more suffering to our original wounds. We tried to protect ourselves by running from the pain, putting on a mask, and pushing people away for fear of being vulnerable, all to adapt to what often feels like a hostile world.

We start to recover when we let ourselves believe in and rediscover our pure, radiant, and courageous heart where we find our potential for awakening resides. Who were we before the world got to us? Who are we beyond the obsession of our conditioned minds? Who are we beneath all our walls and heartbreak? Despite the trauma, addiction, fear, and shame, there is a still and centered part of us that remains whole. There is a part of us that's not traumatized, that's not addicted, that's not ruled by fear or shame. This is where wisdom comes from, and it's the foundation of our recovery.

If you're at the beginning of your recovery journey, it may seem impossible to access this part of you. But you're here because you already have. Perhaps you felt some small glimmer of hope — maybe born out of desperation — that there might be a way out, that things could change if you took wise action and reached out for help. Maybe it feels impossible to have faith in this part of you, to believe that you have the potential to be capable of wisdom and kindness and ethical deeds, to believe you can be the source of your own healing and awakening. Recovery is a gradual process. This path is a lifetime of individual steps. It's not only the Buddha's example that shows us the way, but also those before us who have gone through the process of recovery and made it to the other side. They show us that we can, too.

So what does the Buddha have to do with recovery?

There are two ways in which we use the word Buddha, which means "awakened." First, it is the title given to Siddhartha Gautama, a prince who lived in modern-day Nepal and India roughly 2,500 years ago. After many years of scholarly study, meditation, and ethical practice, he was awakened to the nature of human suffering and discovered a path that leads to the end of suffering, and the freedom that comes from awakening. After his awakening, Siddhartha came to be known as the Buddha.

The second use of the word Buddha follows from the first. Buddha can refer, not only to the historical figure but also to the idea of awakening: the fact that each of us has within ourselves the potential to awaken to the same understanding as the original Buddha. When we take refuge in the Buddha, we take refuge not in Siddhartha as a person, but in the fact that he was able to find freedom from his suffering and so can we.

THE STORY OF THE ORIGINAL BUDDHA

To understand the nature of this awakening it could help to know something about the life of Siddhartha Gautama.

One of the many versions of the story of the Buddha tells us that Siddhartha was a wealthy prince, born into privilege, and sheltered from much of the suffering of the world. The story goes that young Siddhartha sneaked away from his palace and saw people suffering from old age, sickness, and death. He realized that no amount of privilege could protect him from this suffering. Wealth wouldn't prevent it. Comfort wouldn't prevent it. Pleasure wouldn't prevent it. Despite having a life of ease, Siddhartha still found that he experienced suffering and dissatisfaction. He was born with everything, but it wasn't enough.

This persistent dissatisfaction with life, whether dramatic or subtle, is called **dukkha**, a Pali word we still use today. All humans experience dukkha, but some of us — particularly those of us who have struggled with addiction — seem to experience it on a more intense level, and with worse consequences.

What is addiction but the consistent and nagging feeling of "not enough?" What is addiction other than being constantly unsatisfied?

Siddhartha saw that pain was an unavoidable part of life, and he became determined to find a way to put an end to it. He left his family and for a time, lived the life of an ascetic — the extreme opposite to his previous life of comfort and wealth. As an ascetic, he sat in extremely uncomfortable postures meditating for long periods of time. He slept very little. He ate very little. He even tried breathing very little. He thought that, since material comfort hadn't eliminated suffering, maybe the opposite of material comfort would. At the brink of death, Siddhartha abandoned the idea of extreme asceticism and instead chose what he called "the middle path."

Siddhartha realized that both the extremes of pleasure and denial of pleasure had brought him nowhere nearer to liberation. Neither extreme had given relief from his suffering. So he set off on his own to meditate. Sitting beneath a Bodhi tree, he meditated deeply and discovered the path that leads to the end of suffering. He looked within himself for his own liberation, and he found it.

What Siddhartha understood as he meditated under the Bodhi tree is known as the **Dharma**, or the "Truth," which explains the causes and nature of cyclical suffering. It's the basis of the teachings of Buddhism. Central to this path are the Four Noble Truths and the Eightfold Path, which will be explained in the next chapter.

Siddhartha was called the Buddha, or "The One Who Woke Up," because most people go through life with a false sense of reality, like being in a trance. The Buddha spent the rest of his life developing the Dharma into a simple but sophisticated system. He shared it with anyone who would listen, dedicating himself to a life of service to free everybody from suffering. He defied the norms of his time by letting women and the poorest class of citizens become monastics. Everyone was welcome in his sangha, his spiritual community. Central to his teachings was the idea that liberation is available to all — to the most broken and oppressed among us, to the sick, to the powerless, to those who have lost everything, to those who have nothing left to lose. All of us, even the most addicted, the most lost, can find our way to awakening, because we all have the ability to access the pure, wise, and true nature within each of us.

WALKING IN THE FOOTSTEPS OF THE BUDDHA

The story of the Buddha may seem far removed from our everyday reality, but his life before and after his awakening offers us a model for our own lives. All of us can relate to the inevitability of suffering. Aging, sickness, and death have touched us all. We've experienced the truth of impermanence — the highs we achieved in our addictions always wore off, but we kept chasing them anyway. We've also endured other forms of suffering, some self-inflicted and some at the hands of others. And we've dealt with subtle forms of dukkha: the annoyances, the boredom, the loss of what we want, the inability to keep what we have, the impatience with life, the refusal to accept what is. And what have we done with these experiences of suffering?

At this point most of our stories start to look different from Siddhartha's, and this difference is what led us here. Instead of sitting with our suffering, we found ways to change it, avoid it, or replace it with something more pleasurable. For some of us, that came in the form of drinking or using drugs. Others used sex, relationships, food, self-harming, technology, work, or gambling. And some of our stories contain a version of "all of the above." Whatever the behavior, it was just a temporary solution that always led to deeper suffering for ourselves and others.

We've come to realize that our stories don't have to continue like this. The life of Siddhartha, and the lives of the countless people we meet in recovery who have found an end to the suffering of addiction, prove to us that there is another way.

We can look back on our own lives and see clearly the path that brought us here. We can examine our own actions and intentions and come to understand how we shape our own future. And we can gain insight into the nature of our own suffering and follow a path that leads to less harm and less suffering.

The Buddha began as a layperson with suffering, just like us. This is not a path of miracle or blind-faith. This is a path of practice and the Buddha can be an ideal that inspires us. Experience has shown us that good results come when we put the necessary effort into our own recovery. This is a program of empowerment: we take responsibility for our own intentions and actions. The Sangha is here to help us along the way.

We don't have to identify as Buddhists, and we don't have to meditate for hours each day. But we have found that the path outlined in the Four Noble Truths and the Eightfold Path can lead us to liberation from both the suffering of addiction and the suffering that comes from simply being human. We trust in the potential in all of us to find freedom from this suffering.

THE TRUTH: DHARMA

As people who have struggled with addiction, we're already intimately familiar with the truth of suffering. Even if we've never heard of the Buddha, at some level we already understand the core of the teachings: that in this life, there is suffering.

It can be incredibly liberating to hear this said so plainly and directly. No one is trying to convince or convert us. No one is telling us we have to believe something. No one is sugarcoating our experience.

The Buddha also taught the way to free ourselves from this suffering. When the Buddha awakened, he understood how samsāra, or the cycle of existence, came to be and how it is maintained. The heart of these teachings (which we call the Dharma) is the Four Noble Truths. These four truths, and the corresponding commitments, are the foundation of our program:

1. There is suffering. We commit to understanding the truth of suffering.
2. There is a cause of suffering. We commit to understanding that craving leads to suffering.
3. There is a way of ending suffering. We commit to understanding and experiencing that less craving leads to less suffering.
4. There is a path that leads to ending suffering. We commit to cultivating the path.

Like a map that shows us the path, these truths help us find our way in recovery.

THE FIRST NOBLE TRUTH:
There is Suffering

Some of the ways in which we may experience suffering are obvious, like poverty, hunger, pain, disappointment, and feeling separated or excluded. There is also suffering due to the divisions of our world, such as war, colonization, and oppression. Some are less obvious, like feelings of cravings, anxiety, stress, and uncertainty. We also suffer as we struggle with birth, aging, sickness, and death. As much as we want to avoid what we consider unpleasant and hold onto what we label as pleasant, dissatisfaction, separation, loss, and injustice still may frequently arise. Suffering occurs whenever we fail to see the true nature of our existence, when we insist on controlling or altering our reality.

The First Noble Truth rests on the understanding that our lives seem unsatisfactory because experiences are impermanent and impersonal. Our senses (which the Buddha understood to include not just hearing, seeing, smelling, tasting, and touch, but also thinking) are often unreliable and temporary, which means that the way we experience and make sense of the world is constantly changing and subjective. We suffer because we keep expecting these temporary experiences to be permanent and absolute, and to satisfy our craving for pleasure or to avoid pain.

Many of us have suffered by trying and failing to control our dependencies, habits, and addictions. We've used every kind of willpower, bargaining, planning, and magical thinking; each time imagining the result would be different, and blaming ourselves when it turned out the same.

How many times did we promise: "Just this one last time, then I'm done? I'll just use or drink on the weekends, or only after work, or only on special occasions. I'll never drink in the morning. I won't do the hard stuff. I'll never get high alone. I'll never use at work or around my family. I'll never drink and drive. I'll never use needles."

How many diets have we tried? How many times have we said we wouldn't binge, or purge, or restrict calories, or over-exercise?

How many times have we looked at the scars on our arms and vowed to never cut again? How many times have we let our wounds heal, only to break them open once more?

How many limits have we set on ourselves around technology or work, only to get pulled back in? How many times have we vowed to have no more one-night stands, vowed to stay away from certain people or places or websites? How many times have we crossed our own boundaries and been consumed by shame?

How many mornings did we wake up hating ourselves, vowing to never do again what we did last night, only to find ourselves repeating the same mistake again just a few hours later?

How many times did we attempt to cure our addictions with therapy, self-help books, cleanses, more exercise, or by changing a job or relationship? How many times did we move, thinking our shadow wouldn't follow us?

How many promises did we make? How many times did we break those promises?

Having suffered and struggled with addiction in its many forms, we've come to understand this first truth as it relates to recovery: Addiction **is** suffering. We suffer when we obsess, when we cling and grasp onto all of the delusions of addiction, all the impermanent solutions to our discomfort and pain. We've tried to cure our suffering

9

by using the very substances and behaviors that create more discomfort and pain. All our attempts to control our habits demonstrate how we've been clinging to the illusion that we can somehow control our experiences of the world or how others have treated us. We're still trapped in the prison of suffering. In fact, we're reinforcing its walls every time we act on our addictions.

Liberation comes when we gain a clear understanding of where our real power lies, and when we are throwing it away.

This is a program of empowerment. It's a path of letting go of behavior that no longer serves us and cultivating that which does.

TRAUMA AND ATTACHMENT INJURY

Many of us have experienced trauma, often described as the psychological damage that occurs after living through an extremely frightening or distressing event or situation. For some of us, this trauma can be a long-term experience. It's caused by an overwhelming amount of stress that exceeds our ability to cope, and may make it hard to function even long after the event. Trauma can come from childhood experiences or from events that occur in our adulthood. It can be sudden, or it can develop over time from a series of events that changed how we perceive ourselves and the world. This also includes the resulting trauma from discrimination and bigotry. While trauma frequently comes from life-threatening events, any situation that leaves one feeling emotionally or physically in danger can be traumatic. It's not the objective facts of the event that define the trauma; distress is relative and what might be considered traumatic for one may not be for others. Generally, the more terror and helplessness we feel, the more likely it is we'll be traumatized.

Attachment injury can be just as insidious and harmful as trauma, and can have the same impact. It's defined as an emotional wound to a core relationship with a caregiver, often caused by abuse, neglect, or inconsistency of care in early childhood.

Trauma and attachment injury can impact our recovery and meditation practice in slightly different ways. With trauma we may feel fear (even panic) or distrust when asked to "sit" in meditation, even when intellectually we know we're in a safe place with a supportive group. It may be triggering to be asked to be present in our bodies and minds, or to focus on our breath. It might also feel unsafe when your identity is uniquely different from the majority of the sangha.

Attachment injury may show up as a hesitation to trust people or a process, as a reluctance to be part of a recovery group or sangha, or as a core belief that we don't belong. In this case, the nurturing thing to do for ourselves might be to lean into this discomfort, compassionately engage, and investigate the stories we're telling ourselves about not belonging. Again, it's key to become aware of the nature of the harm we carry with us. Trauma and attachment injury may require different ways of feeling safe and supported. You should always do whatever is most compassionate for yourself in the moment, and seek outside help when you need it.

Trauma and attachment issues are relevant to suffering and addiction because they can have a huge impact on our mental and physical health. Studies show that those who struggle with addiction have often experienced trauma at some point in their lives. What we try and use to make us feel better, whether it's substances or behaviors, often only reinforces the cycle of aversion and craving that will lead to more suffering. The brain can be overactive when trauma is present because it perceives a very real threat, and the body often responds with feelings of helplessness, fear, and vulnerability. This system can be easily thrown into overdrive when one's life experience screams: "You're not safe! Danger! Danger!" Even when the danger is no longer present.

For some people, post-traumatic symptoms may be increasingly severe and last long after the original events have ended. Many of us have intrusive thoughts that seem to come out of the blue, or we feel confusion or mood swings we can't link to specific events. Traumatic responses may lead us to avoid activities or places that trigger memories of the event. We can become socially isolated and withdrawn, and lose interest in things we used to enjoy. Post-Traumatic Stress Disorder (PTSD) may cause us to be easily startled, edgy, have impaired function during sex or other activities, or unusually alert to potential danger.

Overwhelming fear, anxiety, detachment and isolation, shame, and anger may become background states of our activities. Many other effects of trauma may be triggered by social interactions, work, or meditation — areas that may be completely disconnected from the original events.

Race-based trauma, as well as trauma from any experience of discrimination or bigotry, can accumulate over a lifetime. When these incidents are considered separately, they might appear manageable, but when experienced cumulatively, they can become extremely difficult to cope with. The distress, fear, and physical body responses that may arise from this kind of trauma often overlap with the symptoms of PTSD.

Trauma and attachment injury can lead to the fear, anger, anxiety, guilt, and loneliness that are common responses to various life experiences. But, at a deeper level, trauma makes it harder for us to cope in general, to form healthy or safe relationships, to develop an identity in the world, or to defend ourselves. No two of us will react to the same experience in the same way, but this truth points to the fact that certain past experiences can affect our responses later in life. This is key to understanding dukkha, and to meeting our experience with wise-boundaries, compassion, kindness, and courage rather than judgment (for others and ourselves), which is an essential part of recovery.

Many of us turned to addictive substances and behaviors as a way to cope with our trauma. Sometimes running from the pain of our experiences by way of our addictions was itself a survival technique from feeling that we wouldn't be able to live through the pain of our memories. While this may have provided some temporary relief, it did nothing to actually heal the pain of our trauma, and often led to even more pain.

Our trauma is not our fault, but healing from it is our responsibility, and our right. Developing understanding and compassion toward the way trauma affects our reactions to events or circumstances in the present moment is an important part of that healing.

INQUIRY OF THE FIRST NOBLE TRUTH:

- Begin by making a list of the behaviors and actions associated with your addiction(s) that you consider harmful. Without exaggerating or minimizing, think about the things you have done that have created additional suffering to yourself and others.

- For each behavior listed, write how you and others have suffered because of that behavior.

- List any other costs or negative consequences you can think of, such as finances, health, relationships, sexual relations, or missed opportunities.

- Do you notice any patterns? What are they? What are the ways that you might avoid or reduce suffering for yourself and others if you change these patterns?

- How have your addictive behaviors been a response to trauma and pain? What are some ways you can respond to trauma and pain that nurture healing rather than avoidance?

- If you have experienced trauma from discrimination, what are ways you can experience healing and practice self-care? Consider opportunities to support social justice while allowing yourself to heal and practice compassion for yourself and others.

THE SECOND NOBLE TRUTH:
The Cause of Suffering

As people who have become dependent on substances and behaviors, we've all experienced the sense of failure and hopelessness that comes from trying, and failing, to let go of our fixations. Addiction itself increases our suffering by creating a hope that both pleasure and escape can be permanent. We go through this suffering again and again because substances or behaviors can only give us temporary relief to our pain, our unhappiness, and our lost or damaged sense of self.

Our refusal to accept the way things are leads to wanting, or craving, which is the cause of suffering. This excludes discrimination-based suffering and harm which do not need to be "accepted" but met with wise boundaries, wise action, and compassion. We don't suffer because of the way things are, but because we want — or think we "need" — those things to be different. We suffer because we cling to the idea that we can satisfy our own cravings, while ignoring the true nature of the world around us. Above all, we cling to the idea that we can hold on to impermanent and unreliable things, things that can't ever lead to real satisfaction or lasting happiness, without experiencing the suffering of one day losing them.

Clinging to impermanent solutions for suffering results in craving. We experience craving like a thirst, an unsatisfied longing, and it can become a driving force in our lives. If craving goes beyond simple desire, which is a natural part of life, it often leads us to fixation, obsession, and the delusional belief that we can't be happy without getting what we crave. It warps our intentions so that we make choices that harm ourselves and others. This repetitive craving and obsessive drive to satisfy it leads to what we now know as addiction. Addiction occupies the part of our mind that chooses — our will — and replaces compassion, kindness, generosity, honesty, and other intentions that might have been there.

Many of us experience addiction as the loss of our freedom to choose; it's the addiction that seems to be making our choices for us.

In the way we "must have" food, shelter, or water, our mind can tell us we "must have" some substance, buy or steal something, satisfy some lust, keep acting until we achieve some "needed" result; that we must protect ourselves at all cost and attack people with whom we disagree, or people who have something we want. This "need" also leads to an unsettled or agitated state of mind that tells us we'll only be happy if we get certain results or feel a certain way. We want to be someone we're not, or we don't want to be who we are.

Conditions or circumstances in and of themselves don't cause suffering. They can cause pain or unpleasant experiences, but we add suffering on top of this when we think we "need" those circumstances to be different. We create even more suffering when we act out in ways that deny the reality of the circumstances and the reality of impermanence. Craving is the underlying motive that fuels unwise actions that create suffering.

INQUIRY OF THE SECOND NOBLE TRUTH:

- List situations, circumstances, and feelings that you have used harmful behavior to try to avoid.

- Name the emotions, sensations, and thoughts that come to mind when you abstain. Are there troubling memories, shame, grief, or unmet needs behind the craving? How can you meet these with compassion and patience?

- What things did you give up in your clinging to impermanent and unreliable solutions? For example, did you give up relationships, financial security, health, opportunities, legal standing, or other important things to maintain your addictive behaviors? What made the addiction more important to you than any of these things you gave up?

- Are you clinging to any beliefs that fuel craving and aversion, beliefs that deny the truth of impermanence, or beliefs about how things in life "should" be? What are they?

- If you have experienced discrimation-based trauma or social injustice, how can you meet the experience in a way that honors your true self, without creating more pain and suffering?

THE THIRD NOBLE TRUTH:
Ending the Suffering

It is possible to end our suffering. When we come to understand the nature of our craving and realize that all our experiences are temporary by nature, we can begin a more skillful way to live with the dissatisfaction that is part of being human. We don't need to be torn apart by our thoughts and feelings that say, "I have to have more of that," or "I'll do anything to get rid of this." The Third Noble Truth states that the end of craving is possible. Each of us has the capacity for recovery.

We are responsible for our own actions and for the energy we give our thoughts and feelings. This means we have some control over how we respond to our own suffering, because the unpleasant emotions take place within us; we create them through our response to experience. We don't need to depend on anyone or anything else to remove the causes of our suffering. We may not be able to control anything "out there," but we can learn to choose what we think, say, and do. We come to understand that if our thoughts, words, and actions are driven by greed, hatred, or confusion, we are creating suffering within suffering. If we let go of these attitudes, we can lessen suffering or even create freedom. We can choose to give up these causes of disturbing and unpleasant emotions. This is the true empowerment and freedom of recovery — recognizing that happiness and suffering are up to us, based on how we choose to respond to our experiences.

INQUIRY OF THE THIRD NOBLE TRUTH:

- What makes it so hard to quit?

- What resources are available to help you abstain and recover?

- List reasons to believe you can recover. Also list your doubts. What might the wise and compassionate part of you — your Buddha nature — say about these doubts?

- Practice "letting go" of something small. Notice that the craving doesn't last and that there's a little sense of relief when you let it pass. That's a little taste of freedom.

THE FOURTH NOBLE TRUTH:
The Path

The Buddha taught that by living ethically, practicing meditation, and developing wisdom and compassion, we can end the suffering we create by resisting, running from, and misunderstanding reality.

The Fourth Noble Truth is the Path that summarizes the essential elements to recovery, or awakening, and leads to the ending of suffering. It provides an instructive practice for investigating and becoming aware of the conditioned responses we cling to. These are the eight factors of the Path:

1. Wise Understanding
2. Wise Intention
3. Wise Speech
4. Wise Action
5. Wise Livelihood
6. Wise Effort
7. Wise Mindfulness
8. Wise Concentration

These eight factors can be divided into three groups:

- The Wisdom group of Understanding and Intention.
- The Ethics group of Speech, Action, and Livelihood.
- The Concentration group of Effort, Mindfulness, and Concentration.

Each of us will understand and practice each aspect of this Eightfold Path in our own way. We develop our wisdom, ethical practice, and concentration as far as we can in any given moment. As we come to a deeper understanding of the Four Noble Truths, we're able to bring more effort and concentration to letting go of our greed, hatred, and confusion. Our ethical development will cause us to reflect more deeply on these sources of our unwise actions.

The Eightfold Path is a way of life that each of us follows and practices to the best of our current understanding and capacity. The Path can serve as both a religious and non-religious journey. For many people, their Buddhist practice includes prayer, worship, and ceremony. It is up to you to decide whether to include these practices as part of your recovery path.

INQUIRY OF THE FOURTH NOBLE TRUTH:

• Understanding that recovery and the ending of suffering is possible, what is your path to recovery and ending the suffering of addiction? Be honest about the challenges you might face, and the tools and resources you will use to meet those challenges.

• What behaviors can you change to more fully support your recovery?

• What does it mean to you to take refuge in the Buddha, the Dharma, and the Sangha for your recovery?

THE EIGHTFOLD PATH

We've found that it's useful to make inquiry and investigation a normal part of our everyday routine, especially when we're feeling uncomfortable emotions or facing tough decisions. We can take a moment to pause and sit with what we're experiencing, identify it, and simply allow it to be, with compassion and without judgment. Then use the Eightfold Path as a guide to go inward and forward by asking ourselves: "How can I apply the Eightfold Path?" It can also be beneficial to use the different sections of the Eightfold Path as an end-of-day reflection.

WISE UNDERSTANDING

As we engage in the world, rather than withdraw from it, we can use Wise Understanding to live without clinging, attachment, or craving. By paying attention to our actions and the results of those actions, we can begin to change where our choices are leading. If we intend to act in ways that have positive results, and if we're aware of the true intention and the nature of our actions, then we'll see better results — better meaning less suffering and less harm.

The word *karma* in Sanskrit translates to "what our actions create." Any intentional act — mental, verbal, or physical — is a kind of karma. Skillful or wise actions strengthen our sense of balance, kindness, compassion, loving, and equanimity. When we act unskillfully or unwisely — when we steal, lie, take advantage of somebody else, or cause intentional harm based on our own craving or delusions — it creates an immediate sense of imbalance. It fights with our intention to avoid harming others. Karma is determined by our intention and applies to any volitional or purposeful action. The result of our volitional actions may be an increase in our happiness or may lead to additional suffering. There is no actor apart from action, and there is no action without intention.

Unskillful actions leave us less able to meet the next challenge or pain we face. For example, when we steal, we have to immediately justify to ourselves why our greed was more important than the harm we caused by taking. We must create a cover story, hide our actions, and adjust to the fear of getting caught. Ultimately, if the theft gets discovered, we might have to deal with financial or legal consequences, or face a lack of trust from our community. Similarly, when we're dishonest, we immediately focus energy on maintaining the untruth. We must emotionally carry the potential pain that is caused to others, and ourselves, if the lie is revealed.

This understanding of karma rests on the insight that we are responsible for our own happiness and misery, and there is a cause to every experience of happiness or misery. From a Buddhist point of view, our choices — which are dependent on our present mental, moral, intellectual, and emotional conditions — decide the effects of our actions. If we act skillfully, with understanding and compassion, it's possible to cause positive, beneficial effects for ourselves and others. If we act with unskillful intention, we cause our own suffering.

This doesn't mean that we always have control over our experiences. No matter how skillfully we act, the external world — people, places, things, societal structures — might not give us what we want. This does not mean we have "bad karma," or that we've failed. It just means that we're not in control of everything and everyone. The point is that, regardless of what the outside world throws at us, we're responsible for how we respond to it and how we tend to our internal world. At the end of the day, we have the choice whether we go to bed as somebody who acted wisely and compassionately, or as somebody who didn't.

It's important to note that being responsible for our own happiness and suffering doesn't mean we're responsible for pain inflicted on us by others, or by circumstances out of our control. Many of us have experiences of victimization, oppression, and trauma through no fault of our own. The pain from these experiences should be met with compassion, understanding, and wise boundaries, not minimized, invalidated, or pushed away. In recovery, we learn that we don't have to add an extra layer of suffering to this pain. We can begin to heal rather than let these experiences or the action of others control and limit us. Without discounting or ignoring the ongoing effects of trauma in our lives, we begin to understand that our responses when that trauma comes up for us, can change our experience of suffering and happiness.

The Buddhist perspective is that our present mental, moral, intellectual, and emotional circumstances are the direct result of our actions and habits, both past and present. How we choose to respond when confronted with pain or discomfort will change our ability to skillfully deal with suffering when it arises. We can also take solace in the fact that we're not alone, that every person has difficult and unpleasant experiences. It's how we respond to pain that determines our experience.

INQUIRY OF WISE UNDERSTANDING:

- Think of a situation in your life that is causing confusion or unease:
    1. What is the truth of this situation?

    2. Are you seeing clearly, or are you getting lost in judgment, taking things personally in stories you're telling yourself, or repeating past messages you've internalized? How?

    3. Is your vision clouded by greed, hatred, confusion, clinging, attachment, or craving? How?

- In what situations and parts of your life do you have the most difficulty separating wants from needs? Are there areas or relationships where the drive to get what you desire overshadows any other consideration? Has this changed since you began or continue in recovery?

- Are there parts of your life where you are driven to continue unpleasant experiences because you think you "must" or "need to?"

- How is karma — the law of cause and effect — showing up right now?

- Where in your life are you dealing with the effects or aftermath of action you took in the past, both positive and negative?

WISE INTENTION

Wise Intention describes the attitude or approach we take toward ourselves and the world. We can choose non-harming by avoiding actions that have harmful results, detaching from the cravings that seem overwhelming in the moment, and developing a kind and compassionate stance toward ourselves and the world. Wise Intention leads us to stop doing things based on confusion, ill-will, hatred, violence, and selfishness. It impacts all our relationships: with ourselves, other people, our community, and the world as a whole.

Wise Intention is deciding to act in ways that produce good karma and to avoid actions that produce bad karma. We start by looking at the kinds of thoughts that cause us to act in wise or unwise ways. If our thoughts are based on confusion, fear, and greed, then our actions will bring bad results and create harm. If our thoughts are based on generosity, compassion, and avoiding clinging, then our actions will bring good results. Thoughts that are based in lovingkindness and goodwill, that are free from the desire or intention to cause harm, lead us to act in a beneficial manner.

There may be times when we don't necessarily want to act in a beneficial manner. We may know the right thing to do, but just don't want to do it. It's in these moments we can focus on our intention. Maybe we aren't ready to do the difficult thing, to quit a certain behavior, to set a boundary, or forgive someone for whom we hold a resentment. But we can set the intention to do so, and investigate our willingness in meditation by repeating statements like "May I have the willingness to forgive.... May I have the willingness to quit smoking (or skip that piece of cake, or stay off the internet tonight, etc.).... May I have the willingness to make amends to my partner."

The first choice we can make in Wise Intention is that of generosity. Generosity teaches us how to let go of our self-centeredness, to let go of clinging to ideas of "mine" and "me." Selfishness, or self-centeredness, is one of the ways we justify and cling to our addictive behaviors. Generosity comes from the awareness that we're holding on too tightly to our selfishness. The karmic result of looking at the world only through the lens of "me" and "mine" and "what I want" leads to loneliness, separation, and dissatisfaction. Letting go of this clinging can be the solution.

Letting go of "me" and "mine" does not mean you need to stop acknowledging your social identities within your community.

Without generosity, the mind is confined to a small, tight space. Anything that's not about "me and mine" is off limits. At times in our lives when we become dependent, our world becomes focused on satisfying our cravings, on holding onto what we want right now. We get sucked into the reactivity of survival mode, believing that we must have our addictive substance or behavior to survive. Our "needs" for relief or pleasure consume us, and we become blind to the needs of those around us. We may even begin to see them as threats.

We can break out of this cycle by opening our hearts: by being present for, and in service to other people. Generosity allows space to respond to those around us, to include their well-being in our choices. This can, of course, be a tricky concept for those of us who struggle with issues of codependency. Generosity does not mean giving of ourselves without boundaries until we are depleted. It does not mean using "helping" as a form of manipulation to get what we want. Again, what's important here is that we're honest about the *intention* behind our actions.

We try not to confuse intent with impact. Our intention may be to not harm, but sometimes the impact is that someone feels hurt. Many of us have experienced this in our addictions. Without intending to, and often without even being aware of it, we've created harm in other people's lives. The way we choose to practice compassion in recovery is by being accountable when our actions hurt someone, and by acknowledging this hurt without blame or shame, defensiveness or justification. This includes when we offend someone by inadvertently using unwise speech or actions in regards to their social identity, such as race or gender. In these moments, it is important to recognize the difference between intent and impact, and having a deep appreciation and compassion for the interconnectedness among us all.

Generosity allows us to cultivate **appreciative joy**, which is one of the four **heart practices** of Buddhism, along with compassion, lovingkindness, and equanimity. Joyful appreciation is simply being happy when somebody else has good fortune, happiness, and peacefulness. Generosity lets us appreciate the happiness of others rather than having feelings of envy, jealousy, or wanting them to be just a bit less happy so we seem a little happier by comparison. We want the other person's happiness to increase, for them to become more at peace, and so we learn to appreciate those things in their lives. In the moment of giving, of generosity, we've let go of self-centered desire and grasping what is "mine," or what brings me pleasure. We're giving up any ill-will or aversion we feel toward the person and toward the world. Instead of creating separation and withdrawal, we're actively fostering appreciation for the closeness and connectedness of the world.

This is a joy that's not obstructed by selfish desires, envy, or resentment. It's the purity of happiness for someone else's good fortune. We can choose to cultivate this feeling of joy in the happiness and success of others, without the need to compete or compare. It's actually a feeling that's natural to humans, but it's often neglected when our attention is focused on selfish craving. This is the true seat of generosity: delighting in the happiness of others, without needing anything in return.

The second heart practice is **compassion**, which is first of all a willingness to come close to pain: to recognize it, honor it, acknowledge it, and respond to it wisely. This isn't easy, because just as we want to run from or suppress our own pain, we also want to avoid being with the pain of others. Compassion means sitting with our own pain and that of others. It stops the cruelty of indifference. Compassion for ourselves is crucial. Self-compassion is the key to healing the shame and guilt that we often feel as we begin to recognize the harms we caused through our addictions. You may also find that compassion is difficult to realize when it comes to those who have caused you great harm. In these cases, it can be helpful to focus on your own healing by practicing self compassion, engaging in wise reflection of the Four Noble Truths, and committing to the practices of the path. With time, you may gradually wish for the relief of suffering for those who have hurt you.

Compassion is not just offering sympathy and a helping hand. It's also an intention to avoid causing harm to others and ourselves. This is where we can most easily see the difference between skillful and unskillful actions, and between wise and unwise intentions. Cruelty — and all the harm it creates in the world — comes from a lack of compassion. Cruelty is a desire to cause pain. Compassion is caring about the welfare and happiness of others. Compassion rests on the renunciation of harming living beings and is not only the wish, but also the intention to put an end to their suffering. We need to open our hearts — not just our minds — to all the suffering that is experienced in the world. Compassion is not only a feeling: it is an action.

The third heart practice is **lovingkindness**, also known as *metta*. These are thoughts that are free from ill-will, simply wishing that somebody else be happy, that they be well, and free from suffering. It's the choice to consider the well-being of everyone in how we interact with the world. Metta isn't conditional: it isn't something we offer only to people we like. We can have concern and care even when we're feeling our own pain. We can bring metta to mind when we're faced with difficulty or torn by conflicting feelings about the conditions of life at the moment. Metta doesn't depend on people acting in a certain way, on our feeling a certain way in the moment, or on the result of our caring. It frees us from only caring about the well-being of others when we think it will lead to some outcome. With metta, we don't ask the question "Will it do any good to care about this person's well-being?"

This means that how we think about another person isn't based on their behavior, or even on the other person at all. How we think about a person is up to us—and if it's shaped by the practice of metta, then we can care about every person's well-being, even the most difficult and unpleasant people we know. We can honestly hope that everyone finds a way to be happy without causing harm. Wishing this goodwill towards others frees us from the reactivity and anger that can come when we focus on the person's behavior or what we think they "ought" to do. We can begin to see the suffering and pain that somebody experiences as a result of their actions, and care about that pain even if it might also lead to pain for us or for others. Our wish is that all beings are free from pain and suffering, that they escape hatred and fear, that they are at ease, and that they find happiness.

Generosity, compassion, and lovingkindness make forgiveness not only possible, but also essential for recovery. Forgiveness rests on understanding and caring about the pain and confusion that give rise to actions that we experience as harmful. We forgive when we focus on the person, rather than the action. We forgive only in the present when our hurt and anger make us aware that our resentment is blocking our own compassionate and generous responses. Forgiveness is not so much something we are giving to the person who hurt us, but something we give to ourselves. It's centered more on our own conscious intention in how we choose to respond to them. Just as we sometimes act out of fear, greed, or confusion, we see that others do too. Forgiveness doesn't mean we accept or tolerate harm. It comes from understanding and accepting that the person causing us harm is doing so from a place of pain and confusion. We extend compassion and goodwill to that person, even as we actively try to end the harm. This may mean creating safe boundaries or removing ourselves from exposure to harm. But we do this from a place of compassion and understanding, not resentment.

It is *essential* that we extend the healing of forgiveness and comp assion to ourselves. Forgiveness allows us to let go of the guilt and shame of our own harmful actions. We remember that compassion is an action, so when we forgive ourselves we also set an intention not to re-create or continue the harm we have caused to others and to ourselves.

Making amends is an important part of forgiveness. As we begin to gain clarity about the harm we caused in our addiction, we commit to make amends for that harmful behavior. We don't make amends for the sake of satisfying some external standard of morality, to be forgiven, or to get something in return. Instead, we use the process as a way to let go of our expectations and disappointments in others and ourselves — in other words, to let go of our attachment to a different past.

One of the central principles of karma is realizing that I alone am responsible for the way my past actions impact my *current* responses to the world. We change our habits by letting go of the past and restoring balance in our relationships. Things we did in the past create patterns of behavior that continue to shape our thoughts and intentions in the present. That process doesn't stop until we change our relationship with those patterns, and toward the people we've harmed. Amends are about restoring the balance in our relationships, not about asking for forgiveness from others. In a sense, it is an action we take to forgive ourselves.

When we have come to understand and face the reality of our impact on others, we begin to understand the purpose of making amends. Practicing compassion leads to a desire to relieve the suffering of people we've harmed, and a commitment to not cause further suffering. Even if the person isn't a part of our lives any longer, it's possible to acknowledge their hurt and to offer them our goodwill and our remorse. Making amends means we do what we can to remedy the harm or wrong. If that is not possible, we resolve to do some good, not as compensation, but to develop our habits in a different direction. When we intentionally take responsibility for our actions, we let go of harmful avoidance and self-judgment and develop a sense of connectedness, peace, and ease. Amends begin with a willingness to forgive ourselves and take the path of reconciliation: not only with those we have harmed, but also with our own hearts and minds.

Generosity, compassion, lovingkindness, and forgiveness allow us to experience equanimity as we face pain and discomfort, both in ourselves and others. The fourth heart practice is **equanimity**. During our addictions, we often responded to situations that caused us anger, fear, or resentment with a craving that the situations be different. We gave up and surrendered to the negative experience of life. Equanimity does not mean giving up; it is more a quality of leaning in. It is finding peace exactly where we are, regardless of external circumstances. Equanimity allows us to be right in the middle of things, to understand and accept things as they are without needing to escape. When we gave up, we said, "I don't care what happens." Equanimity, on the other hand, is being able to say, "I can be present for this." It's the acceptance that while there are some things we cannot change, we still have power over how we respond to them. While we don't always have control over our thoughts and feelings, we do have power over how we feed them.

INQUIRY OF WISE INTENTION:

- What compassion or forgiveness can you offer when someone's intention is good but their impact is harmful? If it doesn't feel safe or appropriate to offer this directly to the person, how can you bring that forgiveness into your own heart so you don't have the burden of carrying it?

- During your periods of addictive behavior, how did you act in ways that were clinging, uncaring, harsh, cruel, or unforgiving? Toward whom (including yourself) were these feelings directed? How might generosity, compassion, lovingkindness, and forgiveness have changed your behavior?

- What actions have you taken that have harmed others? Have you formed an intention to reconcile with both yourself and the person or people you've harmed (to make amends)? If so, have you found a wise friend or mentor you can go to for guidance and support in the amends process, (which is summarized below)? What support can this person provide as you begin the process of amends?

MAKING AMENDS:

- Have you done something intentionally that you now recognize caused harm to another? Who has been harmed by your actions?

- Have you honestly formed the intention not to repeat harmful actions and to learn from the experience in future interactions? Have you begun the process of directly addressing the harmful actions of your past?

- Making amends depends on the circumstance, including your present relationship to the person and the extent to which you can undo the harm caused through direct actions (like correcting a public dishonesty or compensating another for things you have taken that were not freely offered). Ask yourself, "What can I do in the present?"

- Can you address and reconcile with the harm you have caused without forming an attachment to being forgiven? Identify the motivation for making each amends.

- What actions would restore balance in your own feelings and approach to whatever harm you have caused? Can these steps be taken without causing new harm to the person or the relationship?

- If you're experiencing a difficult situation or choice in your life right now, investigate the intention you are bringing to this situation:

    1. Are you being selfish or self-seeking? How?

    2. Are you being driven by aversion (running away from an un pleasant experience) or craving (grasping for pleasure)? How?

    3. How could you bring in a spirit of generosity, compassion, lovingkindness, appreciative joy, and forgiveness to this situa tion?

    4. How would this situation look different if you brought these factors to mind before reacting or responding?

    5. If you don't want to, can you at least have the intention and willingness to do so?

WISE SPEECH

Wise Speech is based on the intention to do no harm. We've all used speech in a manner that may create harm: lying to keep others from knowing what's really going on; gossiping with the intention of putting someone down or satisfying our desire to be recognized; stealing time and attention by chattering on and on; or trying to convince others to meet our own needs at the expense of their own. Wise Speech includes all the ways we use our voices, including online and in writing.

The basic foundation of Wise Speech is honesty or truthfulness. Dishonesty is exaggeration, minimizing, omitting or lying with the intention of presenting a distortion of reality. It can take the form of "white lies" to avoid embarrassment or exposure, half-truths to keep from being caught, or seemingly harmless things said at the expense of others. We may say more than we really know to be true in the hopes of appearing smarter or more confident in our position or feeling. Sometimes we say something before we know the truth.

Dishonesty has to do with our intention in speech. Are we motivated by greed, fear, or confusion? Or are we motivated by a sincere desire to express what's true, what's useful, what's kind, and what's timely? Wise Speech means we speak with the intention of not causing harm, and of fostering safety and security in our community.

In active addiction, we develop the habit of dishonesty. We lie to cover up or mislead others about the nature and extent of our using or behavior. We lie so we can satisfy the craving our fixation feeds, by hiding our actions, our feelings, or the amount of money and effort we put into satisfying our craving. Many of us lie just for the sake of lying because the truth represents a reality we can't tolerate. We get trapped by our secrets, and for many of us, having a double life becomes an addiction all its own. This is why honesty is foundational to recovery. Dishonesty is one of the habits that allow our addictive behaviors to flourish. As a result, recovery needs to start with an honest appraisal of exactly what lies we told and what dishonesty we spread during our addictive behavior.

The Buddha provided some guidelines for Wise Speech, in addition to truthfulness. He said to avoid slander and gossip, recognizing that such unwise speech causes conflict and makes the community less safe. So, when we talk about others, we can ask ourselves: What's our intention? Is it to cause division or exclusion? Is it to cause shame or embarrassment in someone else, or to somehow make ourselves look better at somebody else's expense? It's possible to talk about other people with the intention of kindness, generosity, and compassion, to seek understanding or support for another. Gossip and slander do not contribute to this and instead, cause harm. Similarly, idle chatter and saying things just to be heard or recognized, or to take up time when we're uncomfortable, can lead people to dismiss or ignore us and may create impatience and intolerance in our community.

Wise Speech is also reflected in the *tone* we use when we talk. If we express ourselves in harsh, angry, or abusive ways, we may not be heard even if we're being truthful. Speaking gently, with the intention of kindness, fosters a community of friendliness and safety. There are always exceptions, of course, and Wise Speech also includes using a loud and strong voice when you need to protect your safety.

It may sound like Wise Speech is primarily about discerning when not to speak, but this isn't always the case. Many of us grew up in families where it wasn't safe to talk openly about our thoughts and feelings. Some, because of certain experiences or cultural conditioning, have been taught that we don't have permission to use our voices or lack the power to speak and be heard. For many of us, practicing Wise Speech may mean learning how to use our voices that have been silenced, and to wisely communicate the needs and boundaries we've gotten used to keeping hidden. At times, this includes speaking up for others when harm is done. Many of us, in an effort to be liked, for fear of rocking the boat, or due to the exhaustion of repeatedly not being seen and heard, have favored being nice over being honest and true to ourselves. Wise Speech teaches us that speaking up, even when it's hard, is sometimes the best choice, and that speech is never truly kind if we cause harm to ourselves.

Finally, Wise Speech is *careful listening*. It is also knowing when not to speak when a wise response isn't available to us. We must listen with compassion, understanding, and receptivity. It can be really helpful to observe how much of the time we spend "listening" to someone else is actually spent judging them or planning what we're going to say in response. Deep listening — without selfishness, or an agenda — is an act of generosity that lets us build true connection.

INQUIRY OF WISE SPEECH:

- Have you caused harm with your speech? How?

- Have you been dishonest or harsh in your communication? When, and in what specific ways?

- Do you use speech now to hurt or control people, to present a false idea or image of yourself or of reality, to demand attention, or to relieve the discomfort of silence? Detail specific instances in which you used speech to mislead, misdirect, or distract.

- Are you careful to avoid causing harm with your speech?

- Do you say things you know are not true, or pretend to know the truth about something when you don't, to appear more knowledgeable or credible than you are? List some examples.

WISE ACTION

Wise Action is also based in the intention to do no harm and to foster compassion, lovingkindness, generosity, and forgiveness. We try to do what's skillful, and avoid actions that are unskillful. Wise Action asks that we try to make choices based on understanding and not unthinking habits or ignorance.

The Buddha suggested that we make a commitment to avoid five specific actions that cause harm, a commitment which is known as the Five Precepts. We commit to the Five Precepts as our basic ethical system:

1. We set the intention to avoid taking the life of another living being, or from causing harm to ourselves or another living being.
2. We set the intention to avoid taking what is not freely given, or stealing.
3. We set the intention to avoid causing harm through our sexual conduct, and to be aware of the consequences and impact of our sexual activity and desire.
4. We set the intention of being honest, of not lying, and of not using speech in a harmful way.
5. We set the intention to avoid the use of intoxicants and intoxicating behavior that cloud our awareness.

We need to continually reflect on and question the intentions behind our actions. We may have moments of clarity, but these can quickly pass, when old habits or thoughts resurface. We commit to constantly reminding ourselves of our intention to Wise Action: to act in ways that arc non-harming.

INQUIRY OF WISE ACTION:

- Have you acted in a way that was unskillful or that created suffering? How?

- During those times you were unskillful or created suffering, how would it have changed the outcome if you had acted out of compassion, kindness, generosity, and forgiveness? Would you now have a different emotional or mental response to your past actions if you had acted with these principles in mind?

FIRST PRECEPT:

- Have you caused harm? How? Allow for a broad understanding of harm, including physical, emotional, mental, and karmic harm such as financial, legal, moral, microaggression, or any of the "isms" and phobias such as racism, sexism, ableism, classism, homophobia, transphobia, etc.

- Even if you can't point to specific harms that you have caused, have you acted in a way that purposely avoided being aware of the possibility of harm?

SECOND PRECEPT:

- People "take" in many ways: we take goods or material possessions, we take time and energy, we take care and recognition. With this broad understanding of taking, have you taken what has not been freely given? How? What are specific examples or patterns where this has been true for you?

THIRD PRECEPT:

- Have you behaved irresponsibly, selfishly, or without full consent and awareness (from yourself or partners) in your sexual conduct? How?

- Reviewing your sexual partners or activities, have you been fully aware in each instance of other existing relationships, prior or current mental or emotional conditions of yourself and your partner(s), and your own intentions in becoming sexually involved? How or how not?

- Has your sexual activity, both by yourself and with others, been based on non-harmful intentions? Have you entered into each sexual activity with awareness and understanding? How or how not?

FOURTH PRECEPT:
- Have you been dishonest? How?

- What patterns did your dishonesty take? Did you act or speak dishonestly to deny or misrepresent the truth about your own behavior or status?

- Were there particular situations in which your dishonesty was particularly present (for instance: when dealing with your addictive behaviors, in job or professional settings, among friends, with family)? Investigate the source of the dishonesty in each setting: Was it based on greed, confusion, fear, denial? Why were you lying?

FIFTH PRECEPT:
- Have you used intoxicants or other behaviors that cloud your ability to see clearly?

- What substances and behaviors have you become reliant on to change or cloud your awareness? Has this changed over time? Or, if you have periods of abstinence, were your habitual intoxicants or behaviors replaced by other ways to avoid awareness of your present circumstances and conditions? How?

- List ways you might practice the Five Precepts, compassion, lovingkindness, and generosity in your decision-making.

WISE LIVELIHOOD

The final factor in the ethical group is Wise Livelihood, which focuses on how we support ourselves in the world. Again, the intent is to avoid causing harm. For most of us, our work occupies so much of our time and attention, so how we choose to make a living takes on special importance. Understanding the principle of karma, and knowing that unethical activity gives rise to harmful karma, whatever choices or circumstances lead us to a particular job need to be recognized as having karmic consequences.

We try to avoid jobs that give rise to suffering and seek work that does no harm or reduces suffering. The Buddha mentions five kinds of livelihood to avoid: trading in weapons or instruments of killing, trafficking in or selling human beings, killing of other beings, making or selling addictive drugs, or business in poison. We're encouraged to avoid occupations based on dishonesty or injury.

Whatever our job is, we can practice it mindfully, with an intention of non-harm, of easing suffering, and of compassion. This means developing an attitude toward our occupation beyond just the money we make. We can develop an approach of service and caring about the effects of our actions on others, both within and outside our workspaces. Wise Livelihood is not about judging ourselves or others for their choice of work or trying to limit their choices. Instead, we try to understand why and how we engage in whatever occupation we practice. Whatever work we do, we can maintain an intention of benefiting others.

INQUIRY OF WISE LIVELIHOOD:

- Does your job cause harm? What is the specific nature of that harm?

- How can you do your job more mindfully and with an intention of compassion and non-harm?

- Do you bring an understanding of karma and kindness to your job, or do you compartmentalize it and exclude it from awareness of wise action?

- What part does greed play in the choices you make in your livelihood? Does greed get in the way of awareness or compassion?

- How can you be of service in your community?

- How might you bring a spirit of generosity to your life, both in your profession and outside it?

WISE EFFORT

Wise Effort is the first of the concentration group. It means concentrating our effort on understanding and recovery and awakening. Wise Effort isn't based on how much we should meditate, how much service we should do, or how much time we put into healthy activity.

Instead, it's the intention to devote balanced energy to supporting the other parts of the path, particularly wisdom.

The first thing to pay attention to is avoiding situations and states of mind that can lead to unethical, unskillful, or harmful responses. We become more aware of conditions in our lives and investigate our own responses and reactions to those conditions. When we're operating out of greed, ignorance, confusion, or thinking we can get what we want, we need to be aware of that. We put in the effort and energy to understand what circumstances allowed these conditions to arise and how we can begin to move away from those responses.

Energy or effort is also devoted to letting compassion, lovingkindness, generosity, and forgiveness arise when they're not present. If we find ourselves reacting with anger rather than compassion, fear instead of generosity, blame instead of forgiveness, we can ask how we would respond if those positive factors were present, and begin to respond more skillfully. Being hard on ourselves, beating ourselves up, and suffering from perfectionism are all familiar feelings during addiction and recovery. When we shame ourselves for not being good enough, not trying hard enough, not being enough, these are perfect opportunities to practice Wise Effort, to reflect on the question, "In this moment, how can I be kind and gentle with myself?"

In early recovery, we may be most interested in damage control: simply stopping the destruction and demoralization we have suffered through our habitual, unskillful responses to craving. We can begin by awareness of that craving, and learning to make different choices that don't trigger the craving. Sometimes awareness is enough; sometimes that's all the effort we can muster. As we learn more skillful responses to our triggers, we gain space to have more compassion, lovingkindness, generosity, and forgiveness. And as this practice becomes more of a habit, equanimity and peacefulness begin to replace our habits of grasping and selfishness. Pacing ourselves is important, alternating periods of activity and rest. We need to be aware of what our mind, emotions, body, and recovery can handle right now, and avoid the stress that can come from pushing ourselves too far, too fast. We need to avoid those things that put us into unskillful mind-states, and try to do things that return us to a more easeful way of being in the present moment.

Try to remember that whatever your experience is right now, it will pass. Remind yourself that you don't really know how long an unpleasant or painful experience will last. Try to be open to recognizing and investigating the experience while it is present, without interpreting it as a permanent part of your experience. Recognizing that the craving, experience, or thought will pass makes it easier to avoid the impulse to make an immediate, unskillful response.

INQUIRY OF WISE EFFORT:

- What efforts have you made to connect with a wise friend, mentor, or dharma buddy who can help you develop and balance your efforts?

- Think of a situation that is causing you discomfort or unease. What is the nature of the effort you're bringing to the situation? Pay attention to whether it feels balanced and sustainable, or if you're leaning too far in the direction of either inactivity or overexertion?

- Are you dealing with overwhelming desires, aversions, laziness or discouragement, restlessness and worry, or doubt about your own ability to recover? How do these hindrances affect the choices you're making?

- Are you avoiding feelings by checking out and giving up, or through obsessive busyness and perfectionism?

WISE MINDFULNESS

Mindfulness — being present to what's going on in our minds, bodies, hearts, and world — is central to the practice of the Eightfold Path. We learn to be present for the way things are with compassion, without judging them or ourselves. Mindfulness is being aware of whatever is present, noticing it, and letting it pass. It's also remembering that we're on a path leading to our freedom and long-lasting happiness.

Mindfulness asks us to be aware and to investigate, without the reactivity and grasping for control that leads to suffering. We learn to stay attentive to what's happening without having to either react to or deny what's happening. For many of us, our addictions prevented us from being mindful. In fact, that was often the whole point: we used our substances and behaviors to avoid feeling, to avoid being aware, because being aware was painful. But by trying to avoid pain, we often created more suffering. We're now making a different choice — to sit with the discomfort rather than pushing it away or trying to numb it. We can learn to sit with the discomfort in different ways, either by bringing awareness to the physical sensations that affect our bodies or in a more distant, non-attached way, such as naming the emotions while allowing them to arise and cease. We're choosing to respond to it with mindful investigation and compassion, and to trust that it will pass if we let it. We're remembering that there's another way to respond to the difficulties of life.

Our minds can get lost in how we react to experiences. When something happens, we almost immediately begin to create a story, plan, or fantasy about it. We have a thought about an experience, that thought leads to another, and on and on until we're far from a real understanding of the experience itself. Mindfulness is noticing the experience in that moment before we get lost in the judgment of the moment or the stories we spin about it. Rather than blindly following our reactions and responses to an experience, mindfulness allows us the space to choose to respond skillfully and from a place of wisdom and morality.

Mindfulness encourages us to be open to and investigate the painful experiences (and our habitual reactions to those experiences), rather than to deny, ignore, suppress, or run from them. Most of us have been conditioned to be our own harshest critic from early on, especially during our fixations on substances and behaviors. We carry the shadow of that judgment with us, even as we seek recovery, giving ourselves negative feedback and scrutinizing every effort we make, holding ourselves to impossible standards of perfection. Letting go of that inner critic allows us to be mindful in the present of the efforts we are making, mindful of the compassion and lovingkindness we're learning to make a part of our practice and our lives. Remember that we often talk way more harshly to ourselves than we ever would to somebody else. It's useful to notice when we're treating ourselves too harshly, and then shift attention to what we are doing well. We can acknowledge the negative thought, and then gently let it go.

Mindfulness practice is based on the Satipatthana Sutta, or the **four foundations of mindfulness**. The first foundation, **mindfulness of the body**, asks us to bring awareness, attention, or focus on our breath and to bodily sensations. Meditations on the breath and body are focused on this awareness. The second foundation is **mindfulness of feeling and feeling tone**s. This practice involves noticing the emotional tone — pleasure or displeasure — that comes with every sensation, even when the sensation is a thought. It also encourages us to notice when a sensation is neither pleasant nor unpleasant but feels neutral. For example, we can experience inhales and exhales by noticing where in our body we feel the breath most directly. The second foundation instructs us to notice those sensations that are neutral, as well as those that are pleasant or unpleasant.

The third foundation, **mindfulness of the mind**, asks us to notice when attachment — also known as greed or wanting — comes up, and to be aware that attachment arises in the mind. We also learn to notice when the mind is not attached to a particular thought or sensation. The same practice of noticing applies when we become aware of aversion, which we can experience as resistance or even hatred. When aversion isn't present in the mind, we can notice that the mind is free from aversion.

In the fourth foundation of mindfulness, **mindfulness of dhammas**, we begin to simply notice when a thought arises, being aware of it without judgment or evaluation, and allowing it to pass away without holding onto it and without creating a story out of it. Training in the fourth foundation lets us be aware of thoughts arising and passing away, and realizing each will pass when we let go.

Two simple practices can make mindfulness a part of our daily lives. First, we can stop whatever we're doing at any moment, and pay attention to the physical sensation of three in-breaths and three out-breaths. This simple practice grounds our attention in what's present right now, rather than in the voices and critics we carry with us. Shifting from the stories and judgments we constantly create during the day to this simple grounding practice of three breaths gives us the space we sometimes need to return to mindfulness of the present moment.

A second practice is to take time to inquire into the truthfulness of the negative or difficult messages we give ourselves. First, take time to ask yourself whether the message is true. Second, ask how sure you are that it's true. Are you absolutely certain about what may seem like an easy or automatic truth? Third, notice how you feel when you believe the thought: Does it lead to fear, anger, sadness, desire? Finally, reflect on who you'd be without the thought. How would you feel if you weren't caught up in the particular mindset or scenario you're creating?

INQUIRY OF WISE MINDFULNESS:

- What are steps you can take to support a regular meditation practice?

- What are steps you can take to practice mindfulness throughout the day by checking in with yourself about how you're feeling, and pausing before reacting to situations?

- What are steps you can take to sit with your discomfort instead of running from it or running toward temporary pleasure?
- What are steps you can take to question the "truths" that your mind tells you, rather than automatically believing them? Identify specific instanceswhere your mind and perceptions "lied" to you about the truth of a situation, and how being aware of that might have changed your reaction and led to a less harmful outcome.

- Think about times when you felt fear, doubt, or hesitation. Now, let yourself become aware of their temporary nature. How might that awareness have led to an outcome that was less harmful?

WISE CONCENTRATION

The final aspect of the Eightfold Path is Wise Concentration. Meditation practice begins with concentrating on the breath, the body, the emotional tone of the moment, and the processes of the mind, because these things exist in the present moment. If we focus on breath, for example, we're paying attention to the present moment because our breathing is immediate: it's happening *right now*. Breathing is a natural process that doesn't require judgment or interpretation, and so it eases the mind from the need to react.

The purpose of concentration is to train the mind to be focused and undistracted. Most of us, early in meditation practice, are distracted by things around us; like a noise outside the room, a pain or discomfort in our bodies, our own worries or judgments of the experience, boredom or weariness, or thoughts and plans. These distractions can lead to a feeling of unease or restlessness. This is perfectly normal. In our addictions, we nurtured the habit of distracting ourselves and for many of us, it became a survival technique. Concentration meditation gives us the opportunity to meet this habit with kindness and patience rather than resistance.

Concentration, like the rest of the factors of the Eightfold Path, is a practice. As with any practice, it takes time and effort to learn a new way to focus attention. In meditation, simply noting the distraction, accepting that it exists, and then refocusing our mind back to the object of concentration, is the practice. If we become focused on discomfort, thoughts, or plans, we need to first recognize that it's happening, and then become curious about it. Then we can make the choice to refocus — to concentrate on the object of the meditation. Our habitual patterns can seduce us into thinking we're doing it wrong, into judging our practice, or into giving up. Don't let them. When we observe what the mind is telling us and react with compassion, knowing we have the power to recognize it and refocus it, we strengthen our ability to concentrate.

Concentration can be especially helpful in times of craving. Instead of getting lost in the delusion that we must have what we're craving, we can trust that the craving is only temporary and refocus our attention on our intention to act wisely. This may simply be the three-breath pause mentioned earlier, or a more formal sitting meditation concentrating on the breath. We can use concentration meditation to train our minds to focus on a helpful thought in the midst of temporary discomfort and the yearning for a quick fix. This may take the form of repeated phrases to focus and clear the mind, such as metta, compassion, or equanimity meditations. It could also take the form of prayer, chanting, a self-affirmation, a mantra, or another form of focused attention. Concentration practices can often bring a sense of well-being and peace in a time of turmoil. They're a healthy way to return to a balanced, resilient state when we're stressed or agitated.

Sometimes when cravings or unpleasant emotions are particularly strong, moving the body can be the best way to help refocus our energy and find relief. Concentration at those times may mean being focused and mindful about each movement we are making: *this is my foot taking a step, this is my hand reaching for the cup*. After a few minutes of concentration practice, of not giving energy to our craving or obsession, we may find the intensity of the feeling has passed. The more we do this, the more we gain confidence that we have the power to relieve the suffering of our addiction through following this path and committing to this practice.

For trauma survivors, the breath, the heart, and the mind can be potentially overwhelming places to place the attention. So if traditional anchors like breath and body are challenging, ask yourself: What helps you stay present? What helps to calm your nervous system? It might be feeling the floor beneath you, or holding a stone, or looking at a piece of art on the wall. All that you need to be present is to pay attention to something happening right now.

If you feel powerful emotions begin to arise during meditation, there are some simple things you can do to remain present. For example, you can open your eyes rather than keeping them closed, or give yourself permission to back off from the practice you are working on. Do whatever you need to do to take care of yourself should such a state arise, whether that is taking some deep breaths, putting a name on your experience (such as "flashback"), or silently repeating some compassionate phrases to yourself. Learning to turn our attention back and forth between challenging sensations and our own supportive resources is a valuable skill that professionals call titration. You can be gentle with your practice as you are working to develop this skill.

INQUIRY OF WISE CONCENTRATION:

- In what ways do you get unfocused or distracted in meditation?

- What are steps you can take to refocus your mind without judging your own practice?

- Notice what value or learning you could gain by carefully and kindly noticing where your mind has gone, or what has distracted you.

- What are steps you can take to use concentration to see clearly and act wisely?

- What are steps you can take to be kind and gentle with yourself through this process?

COMMUNITY: SANGHA

Sangha is the third of the Three Jewels: loosely translated, it means "community." It's where Buddha and Dharma find their expression, where we're supported in putting those principles into action. It's a community of friends practicing the Dharma together in order to develop our own awareness and to maintain it. The traditional definition of sangha originally described monastic communities of ordained monks and nuns, but in many Buddhist traditions it has evolved to include the wider spiritual community. For us, our sangha is our community of both Dharma practice and recovery.

Our Recovery Dharma sangha is decentralized and peer-led, and meetings should be open, safe, and accessible spaces that try to uphold our core principles of mindfulness, compassion, forgiveness, and generosity. The advice in this chapter comes from the collective experience of hundreds of local groups, and so it's offered in the spirit of friendly guidance rather than direction.

The essence of a sangha is awareness, understanding, acceptance, harmony, integrity, and lovingkindness. Recovery begins when we learn to pay attention to and investigate experience in the present moment. It's through the sangha that we first learn to be fully present — that we stop trying to satisfy our craving and turn to an understanding of our thoughts, feelings, sense experience, and actions that include others. This understanding is fundamentally *relational*. Our actions have consequences on not only our own lives, but also on the people with whom we meet and share experiences. Many of us learned this the hard way — by hurting the ones we loved while we were in active addiction. A core part of our recovery includes making amends to those we have hurt, including ourselves. As we've seen, our recovery includes the wise intention to heal the suffering we have caused others and to act wisely to avoid creating the same suffering in the future.

Sangha provides the opportunity to practice a central part of recovery: *remembering*. Remembering our past suffering and reflecting on our current path supports our recovery and energizes our practice of compassion, lovingkindness, generosity, and forgiveness. Sharing these reflections with others who are also struggling with addictive behaviors helps give us confidence in our own ability to recover our true nature, our potential for awakening. Sangha enlarges our perspective and begins to give us the self-confidence and self-respect that will let us reflect on the ups and downs of recovery without discouragement or hopelessness.

When we feel inspired to practice with wise friends, we can trust them to point out with compassion when we fall short of our intentions, and we can be honest with ourselves.

The teachings of the Buddha clearly stress that this is not just something we can do on our own. And many programs of recovery (including our own) emphasize the importance of going to meetings and working with others in recovery. Not every meeting is going to speak to you; keep trying new meetings until one resonates. It's with the support of others that so many of us have found relief from the suffering and isolation brought on by our addictions. It's through being of service that we've been able to get out of our own heads and experience a more sustainable and authentic joy than our addictions have provided.

Many of us have found that there's a quality to our meditations that's different when practiced with a group. Particularly when we're getting started, it can be easy to give up or space out after a few minutes. Practicing with others can often give us the motivation to stick with it long enough to start experiencing some of the benefits of practice. And through sharing our experience and listening to what others have to say, we can see how we're not alone in a lot of our challenges. This can come as a welcome surprise after years of suffering shame and feeling like an outcast.

Many of us, having habitually isolated ourselves, have found that sharing silence at a meeting creates an atmosphere of trust and can be a calming way to get used to being with others. No one is required to speak or participate in meetings; passing is always an option when it comes time to share. There's never any requirement to believe in anything, to identify yourself in any way, much less to become a Buddhist or serious practitioner. The wisdom and tools are available to everyone, wherever they are on their path.

But not every meeting is going to be a fit for every person. You may live in an area where there are several different options to choose from, or there may be only a single recovery meeting near you, or none at all. Fortunately, there are also online meetings, many of which can be joined by phone. You can also start your own meeting.

However you find them, trust that there are wise friends and a sangha out there for you.

ISOLATION AND CONNECTION

Addiction and addictive behavior can create people without roots. Some of us have been uprooted from our families and from society. We wander around, feeling as though we're not quite whole, because our addictions feed our isolation and loneliness. Many of us come from broken families, feel rejected or have been isolated from society through incarceration or institutionalization. Not all of us have disconnected to that degree, but we do tend to live on the margins, looking for a home, for somewhere to belong. A community of practice, a sangha, can provide a second chance to someone who's become alienated from society, or just a comfortable place to bring all of ourselves, including parts we don't usually share with others. If the community of practice is organized with cultural humility and an open, friendly, compassionate atmosphere, we can find support for our practice and recovery.

In our addictions, we self-medicated or engaged in behaviors that helped us deal with the pain of separation. The relief was temporary, of course, often leaving us more lonely and isolated than before, yet we returned to it again and again. For many of us, it was the only way we knew to relieve the pain. Even in sobriety, when faced with well-meaning but insistent people telling us how to overcome our addictions, the instinct for many of us is to keep to ourselves. It's a habitual way of being in the world that a lot of us share.

It wasn't just getting high, though for a lot of people in this fellowship and outside it, that was the main road we took to escape. There were other traps that snagged us, even if we never struggled with substances: sex, food, self-harm, social media. We may have tried to get help with those compulsions, but often found others minimizing or trivializing them, especially in comparison to drug or alcohol abuse. For those of us whose primary addictions are around behaviors and processes, we may have felt alienated and excluded from recovery itself.

Many of us found ourselves like raw, exposed nerves when we stopped using those ways to escape. And sometimes, the last place we wanted to be was in a room with strangers in a circle of chairs all facing each other, talking about how we can't drink or use or participate in our destructive behaviors anymore. The paradox is that it's in that kind of space, where we're accepted as we are, that we can begin to let go of our reflex to hide.

Many of us lost the ability, if we ever had it, to form relationships without the social lubricant of alcohol or drugs. Sometimes that was because we dealt with rejection, trauma, or loss at an early age and became anxious and avoidant around others. Or maybe we just felt different from everyone else since the day we were born, or came from a small community (or a big family) and got sick of people nosing into our business. Whatever reasons we had to isolate, we got to a point where it stopped serving us. The substances and behaviors we used to protect ourselves began to harm ourselves and others. We drove people away to be safe, and as a result we became even more lonely.

Many of us are perennial outsiders. We've felt abandoned by our own families, schools, religious institutions, the government, and society's marginalization of non-dominant identities. As a result, we came to mistrust organizations and groups, and even the idea of belonging itself. The double-bind there, of course, was that because we never allowed anyone to get to know us, we cut off the possibility of ever belonging.

The Buddha taught that nothing and nobody exists on its own. He said: "Since this exists, that exists, and since this does not exist, that does not exist." We're connected to other people through the way we interact, through the air we share, through our existence together in nature. Trying to ignore or resist this interconnection is basically trying to destroy something which already exists.

This doesn't mean that we're *literally* dependent on others for our life and our existence, but that the life and existence of everybody and everything develops through their relationships with things outside themselves — the food they eat, the environment they live in, the history and the circumstances of their world. It's a great web of being that each of us is connected to without any effort of our own. And being aware of that connection gives us the ability to have meaningful and positive relationships with others. It is a choice each of us has: to decide what we want to do with the reality of our connection.

Sangha, in a very broad sense, means being willing to let other people in, to let them matter. To do that, we have to be willing to allow other people to let us in. When we can even consider the possibility of that happening, there's the potential for us to move toward liberation. And the benefits are felt almost immediately.

All of us, during our development and experience of life, had experiences that have made us doubt our own "voices," or the value or wisdom of expressing those voices. Many of these doubts contributed to the suffering we experienced during addiction and have continued to make it difficult to connect to our own recovery. Our meetings are intended to be places where we can feel safe and comfortable authentically expressing what we really feel and experience. However, many of us, because of past experiences in both social settings and in the recovery community, struggle with this; we often struggle just to understand our feelings and experiences.

Your recovery sangha can be one that focuses on helping and encouraging those many voices. Often, for those of us who identify as BIPOC, LGBTQ, or other non-dominant identities, we may wish to attend affinity meetings with others who share our identities. Affinity meetings can be a good place to start feeling safe, seen, and heard. If you're interested in an affinity meeting that does not exist, we encourage you to start one. Our program is one of empowerment, and that includes the support of collective healing and the cultivation of resilience in order to recover our true nature from the suffering imposed on us.

In the Buddhist tradition, it's not just that we don't have to do this work alone, it's that we *need* the support of others on the path to waking up. In a famous story, the Buddha's cousin and assistant Ananda came to visit him and remarked, "This is half of the holy life: having admirable people as friends, companions, and colleagues." The Buddha disagreed, saying, "Having admirable people as friends, companions, and colleagues is actually the whole of the holy life."

When we come together to talk honestly about ourselves and what happened in our lives, something very powerful can happen. When we see people committing to be who they truly are, with all their imperfections and their longing to be free, our hearts naturally begin to open because their realness allows us to be more real. In their vulnerability, our wise, admirable friends give us the freedom to be vulnerable ourselves and to speak our own truths. So our sangha becomes the place where we are supported and encouraged to stay on the path, even when it's challenging or our progress seems stuck. Our wise friends are, often without words, telling us that if we keep going, so will they.

And that can make all the difference in our lives.

REACHING OUT

For many of us in early recovery, asking for help feels almost impossible. But we have found, as difficult as it can be, that it can literally save our lives and that with practice it becomes easier.

Asking for help is not just important because it can get results. At times, in fact, it might not. Even with a lot of help and support, things can stand in our way. Sometimes, what we want from the world and from ourselves is just more than what's available. However, even if asking for help may not always get us what we want, it will always help get us through. When we practice accepting help from people, we become a little more open and a little less stuck. It's the decision to reach out, as much as the answer we receive, that can give us what we need to move forward.

Nevertheless, that decision is often a heavy lift for us. Many of us have done things during our active addictions that we're not proud of. Some of the decisions we made in the past have far-reaching consequences that continue to impact our lives even after we begin our recovery. We may have worn a mask of competence, or fearlessness, or blamelessness, and the fear of what might happen when we take the mask off may keep us from reaching out. We may be afraid that if we ask people in our lives for help with financial problems, legal trouble, or other issues, we might lose them. We might worry that they will no longer respect us or accept us once the mask is gone, because we fear being revealed as broken, fundamentally flawed people. We may have gotten used to hiding a part of ourselves due to past experiences of rejection. We may even be afraid that there's nothing behind the mask, that we're simply empty underneath.

We practice compassion for all beings, including ourselves, to see the truth beneath those fears — that there is a loving and lovable heart within all of us. We come to see clearly that those around us feel more pain watching us struggle alone than they would if we let them in. And, of course, by shutting people out and refusing to let them see our struggles, we'll often bring about the isolation and loss that we were trying to avoid in the first place. So, in view of our own suffering and the pain we can cause to those closest to us, we can see that asking for help is not selfish. In fact, it is an act of great compassion to ourselves and others.

Those who have shared the pain of addiction and isolation understand fear and shame better than we might imagine. Through listening at meetings and sharing our own experiences, we begin to see how we're not uniquely broken or flawed. And it's often easier to ask for help from someone other than those people with whom we are closest. In meetings, we often practice openness and acceptance in learning how others may have different experiences of hurt and trauma. In addition to the people in our sangha, there may be counselors and other professionals in our community who can be a resource when we need someone with experience and a greater degree of objectivity. Some clinics and universities even offer counseling on a sliding scale, so we may not have to eliminate that option just for financial reasons.

Of course, we know intellectually that our problems become easier to face when we have help, but emotionally we may still feel fear. Again, it's the decision to give it a try that may be more valuable than the outcome itself. We learn that letting people in and being a little more vulnerable are not as frightening as we may have thought. In fact, we may find it less daunting than trying to face our problems alone.

When we make a practice of asking for help, we frequently find that it improves both the quantity and quality of our relationships in general. Even if you don't become personally close with people in your sangha outside of meetings, you may find that you are able to connect with more people on a deeper level, and that could be something entirely new in your life. Even if you are seeking help from a spiritual leader, a therapist, or some other professional, notice how opening up to another person affects how much *you* trust *them*. Is there a deepening of respect and feeling of safety as your ability to be transparent grows? This confidence and security may also bring benefits to your other relationships. Try to notice these changes as they arise, and give yourself credit for taking steps that are often difficult.

It's common to worry that sharing your problems with people will cause them to look down on you, burden them with your baggage, or even upset them. And while we must be honest in acknowledging that may be a risk, we also know that remaining isolated can be a much greater risk to ourselves and to others.

There is great truth in the cliché that burdens are lighter when they're shared. Most of us felt as if an enormous weight had been removed from our shoulders when we made the choice to not be alone with our problems anymore. And as we experience relief, we find that asking for help becomes significantly easier.

When we first come into recovery, we may not immediately have easy access to our inner wisdom. Many of us have been relying on the delusions of fear and shame and reactivity as our guides in life. It takes time to lift those veils, to dig through those layers in order to break those habits and begin to see clearly. For many of us, it takes time to be able to trust ourselves. But we can look to our sangha, our community of wise friends on the path, for guidance and wisdom. When we don't know what to do, when we lose faith that we can make it through this craving, when we're lost in obsession and can't make sense of our own minds and hearts, when the world feels upside down, when we are crawling out of our skin with discomfort, when we have no idea what the next wise step is — this is when we can and must reach out to our sangha for help. Because those in our sangha have gone through what we have. They've made it to the other side. And they can show us how to do so as well.

Many — if not most — recovery meetings are focused on meditating together, reading literature or exploring specific topics, and sharing. There are no requirements for attendance other than a respectful curiosity, and meetings are a great opportunity for newcomers to learn about the program. Sometimes, those who have decided to commit to this program of recovery want more support on the path. This is where the idea of a "wise friend" or "mentor" comes in.

The Buddha talked about four kinds of friends: the helpful friend, the kind of friend who sticks with you through good times and bad, the compassionate friend, and the mentor. A **wise friend** supports us through example, kindness, and compassion. It can be anyone in the sangha who we trust to act as a guide, a supporter, or just a fellow traveler on the path. This relationship may take many forms, but it is one built on honesty, compassion, healthy boundaries, and a shared intention to support one another's recovery.

For some of us, especially newcomers, it's helpful to work with a **mentor**, a wise friend who's been in the program for a while who gives support, is there to reach out to when times get rough, and can help hold us accountable. It's not a formal position; nobody is "certified" or "authorized" to be a mentor. They are just members of the community freely sharing their journey through the Four Noble Truths and Eightfold Path. Anyone may choose to collaborate with someone on their path, understanding that each person must ultimately do the work of recovery. Clear communication about expectations from *both* people is important. There are no strict rules, but if you are asked to help someone else in this way, it's a good idea to have someone who's done it before to support you. It's also strongly encouraged that you commit to the Five Precepts, at least as far as the supportive relationship is concerned.

Many people form study or practice groups in addition to attending regular meetings, in order to give and receive help from wise friends on their path of recovery. Some call these *kalyana mitta* groups, the Pāli term for wise or admirable friends. Some call them "Dharma buddies." Whatever the name, people gather to explore particular aspects of the path in a smaller group, like practicing longer periods of sitting meditation, having sangha retreats, studying Buddhist texts, or listening to recorded Dharma talks. There's no one way to run these kinds of groups, and no special experience is needed to start one. You can experiment for yourself and also look to the experience of established groups for ideas.

There are also groups that have formed to support individuals in writing inquiries or investigations of how their addictive behavior led to suffering. This is a powerful technique for self-discovery and liberation, and like most aspects of this program, there is no one "right" way to do it. Some approach it in the same way as inventories in 12-Step programs, and some don't. The goal is not to cause shame or to dwell on past traumas, but rather to turn toward the pain and confusion we have been running from and learn to meet it with kindness, forgiveness, and compassion. You may consider using the Questions for Inquiry as a starting place for your own exploration.

If you need help, know that you're a part of a broader community of wise friends: the sangha of people using Buddhist teachings to support their recovery. It's strongly encouraged for each person to have at least one wise friend or mentor in their group who they can check in with about their recovery. Especially when we are working with difficult aspects of our pasts, holding safe space will require wisdom and compassion.

At any time, in groups as well as in every aspect of our lives, the reminder is that when in doubt, we can be present and we can be kind.

SERVICE AND GENEROSITY

In Buddhism, *dāna*, or generosity, is the first on the list of good qualities that lead a person to enlightenment.

We often think of generosity in terms of money, and many groups use the word dāna to describe the donations that members give to help support the meeting. Dāna is a Sanskrit and Pali word that connotes the virtue of generosity. In the Buddhist tradition, though, dāna is any act of giving — not just money but also food, time, or our attention – without expecting anything in return. It can also take the form of giving to an individual in distress or need. You may already be familiar with the emphasis that many recovery programs put on service, which is consistent with this ancient teaching. The merit of this practice has been central to many religions and philosophies through the centuries.

Generosity with our time, energy, and attention is not only of benefit to others on this path. In Buddhist thought, it has the effect of purifying and transforming the mind of the giver. As we become more generous, it also helps us loosen the grip of greed and attachment that caused so much of our own suffering. From the first time we mindfully put a couple of dollars in the offering bowl or introduce ourselves to a newcomer after a meeting, we can start to feel the benefit of being generous without asking for thanks. With our meditation practice, we learn through direct experience how our bodies and our wealth are impermanent, and this insight makes us more willing to do good with them while we still have them. Sharing our experience at a meeting, or even simply meditating along with others and offering our silent encouragement and support, is an act of kindness that benefits both ourselves and our sangha.

Many of us have trained ourselves for years to be vigilant about being taken advantage of or "ripped off." In some cases, such vigilance has certainly been justified, and there will always be times when we need to establish healthy boundaries. But as our practice deepens, we're able to do so with an attitude of discernment and compassion. In Buddhist teachings, generosity is not a commandment or a "you should," or an unrealistic standard people are expected to measure themselves by, only to find themselves falling short. It is, instead, an illustration of our true nature, of the open and loving hearts that have always been within us but have been covered up for so long that they were almost lost to us. The practice helps us to recover this original nature.

As we try to cultivate generosity in our meetings and in our lives, we learn to trust our innate kindness, and we build confidence that we can give of ourselves and be safe. We continually examine what we perceive to be our limitations and grow in self-esteem, self-respect, and well-being as we see these limitations for what they are: defensive strategies that may once have been necessary, but which have hardened into the handcuffs of habit. The voice of our attachments may say, "I don't want to put my hard-earned money in that bowl," or "Maybe I'll do this act of service, but I'll stop if people don't show enough appreciation." As we practice generosity, we see these fears more clearly and how they have kept us from growing. We begin to realize that this practice is really about creating more space in our hearts and minds. As we expand our capacity for generosity and compassion our heart-minds become more expansive and composed. This brings us greater feelings of happiness and self-respect, and gives our practice more strength and flexibility to look at the conditions of our lives and our recovery.

We can see the benefits of such a practice when we think about the times when our minds and hearts were closed and protective. We felt on edge, uneasy, and usually didn't like ourselves very much. In that state, we had very few resources to face discomfort or confusion. We were often thrown off balance by even small setbacks. Painful or difficult experiences often overwhelmed us and sent us running for temporary relief through substances and/or behaviors.

As we become more comfortable with a generous, open heart, we experience greater balance and ease. When something unpleasant arises, we don't have to worry that it will overpower us. We have a refuge we can increasingly rely on in times of trouble. And when a pleasant experience arises, we don't cling to it desperately, because we don't actually need it to feel good about ourselves.

We practice generosity to be of service to others, to extend healing and happiness to all beings, and to try in some small way to reduce the suffering in this world. As we continue to work with generosity, we learn that the inner practice of recognizing the emptiness of our attachments and building up resilience is one and the same as the outer practice of giving and service.

RECOVERY IS POSSIBLE

In the pages of this book is a path, a set of principles and practices, that can lead to the end of our suffering and see us through the damage that we piled onto ourselves through our addictions. The path is based on gaining and maintaining *mindfulness* of our feelings, bodies, minds, and experiences. During our journey, we come to accept that we're responsible for our own actions, and that every choice has a consequence. If we act unskillfully or mindlessly, we will experience pain in our feelings, thoughts, and experiences (*karma*), and we may cause harm to others. We begin to recognize that every thought, feeling, and experience is only temporary (*impermanence*), that it will pass if we allow it to, and trusting this can provide a safe harbor in moments of craving or pain. We start to believe that even the most difficult, traumatic, and painful actions and events of our past don't define who we are today, nor do they define the possibilities in our future. It is our choices and actions now that define us.

At the same time, we can start to notice and reflect on experience without getting attached to it or to the stories we tell ourselves about it (selflessness). We come to accept that we can never satisfy all of our desires and cravings. We see this in our struggles with impermanence, with sickness and aging, not getting what we want or or losing what we have, not feeling loved by those we desire or feeling rejected by those whose caring we want the most. We sometimes have to deal with people and situations that are painful or uncomfortable (unsatisfactoriness).

But with clear understanding, we can begin to choose more appropriate actions and responses to our experience, and it is in this choice that we find freedom and relief from suffering. When we act with full awareness of each choice, of even the smallest action, we can begin to notice the motivations behind everything we do. We can begin to ask, "Is this action useful or not? Is it skillful or unskillful?" Whenever we're confused or feel lost, we have meditation tools that we can use to simply return to the present moment, to our experience of the present as it is for us *right now*, and we can check in with our sangha — our wise friends — for added perspective and compassionate support.

So, what do we gain by practicing understanding, ethical conduct, and mindfulness? We're asked to sit with discomfort, to experience it without fear or resistance, and to know that it's impermanent. We learn that dukkha is part of the human condition, and efforts to avoid or deny it lead to more unhappiness and suffering. We've learned that we can never satisfy our desires through sense experiences, through chasing pleasure and trying to hold onto it. Every pleasant sense experience will end and the more we try to hold onto it and turn desire into need or craving, the more we suffer dukkha. We're mindful that dissatisfaction and unhappiness have beginnings. By tracing the dissatisfaction or unhappiness back to its root, we can weed it out of the mind.

We follow the Eightfold Path, which allows us to develop understanding. It teaches us the karmic advantage of compassion, lovingkindness, appreciative joy, and equanimity. We learn the quiet satisfaction of living a more ethical and mindful life.

What we are achieving is what in Buddhism is called **sukha**, or true happiness. This is not the temporary pleasure that comes from a high or other temporary sense experience, but the inner peace and well-being that comes from a balanced, mindful life. It is the opposite of the suffering and unsatisfactoriness of dukkha. Sukha is freedom from hate, greed, and confusion. It is an expansive approach to life, being able to sit with and move through feelings of discomfort, dissatisfaction, and discontent. Many of us have been running from and denying dukkha for a very long time, but we have found that it is only when we stop running that we are able to truly access authentic happiness. We can practice the message:

I am here.
This is the way it is *right now.*
This is a moment of suffering. May I give myself the care I need at this moment.
May I accept this without struggling, but also without giving up.

We've started to learn that mindfulness involves investigating our unskillful actions and choices, both past and present, and choosing to act with more wisdom in the future. Rather than being bogged down by guilt or shame about the past, we can use it as a guide to making different choices in the present. As we devote energy to awakening and recovery, we'll learn to investigate our present and our past with wisdom rather than craving or aversion. We'll experience the growth of trust in our own capacity for, and right to, recovery.

As we get a clearer understanding of what we're doing in our lives, of the choices we are making and the consequences of those choices, we gain the opportunity to develop generosity, lovingkindness, forgiveness, and equanimity. These are central to Buddhist practice, and to our recovery. We learn to give freely, because we understand that clinging to what is "mine" is based on the delusion that we are what we possess, or what we control. We learn to have *metta*, or lovingkindness, toward all beings in the world, whether we know them or not.

We come to understand that our practice isn't just for ourselves, but is based on the interconnectedness and happiness of all living beings. Recovery transforms how we show up for those around us. We can become the compassionate, generous, and wise friend whose calming voice and steadfast support can help others to understand their own struggles and find their own path to healing.

There is no magic bullet, no single action or practice that will end suffering. This is a path composed of a set of practices that help us deal with suffering and respond wisely to our own lives. We cannot escape or avoid dukkha, but we can begin to be more at peace knowing there is a path forward: a path with less suffering, less craving, less aversion, less destruction, and less shame. It's a path without an end. It requires effort and awareness. And we don't have to do it alone.

Recovery is the lifelong process of recovering our true nature and finding a way to an enduring and non-harmful sense of happiness. In recovery, we can finally find the peace so many of us had been searching for in our addictions. We can break through our isolation and find a community of wise friends to support us on our path. We can build a home for ourselves, within ourselves, and we can help others do the same. The gift we give to ourselves, to one another, and to the world, is one of courage, understanding, compassion, and serenity. We all experience growth differently, and at our own pace. But the most important message of this book is that the journey, the healing, can start now for you and for each of us.

May you find your path to recovery.
May you trust in your own potential for awakening.

II.

PERSONAL RECOVERY STORIES

AMY

Like so many of us, I grew up never being taught what to do with my feelings, raised by parents who were never taught what to do with theirs. And like so many of us, trauma scarred my young life. I experienced those traumas alone, with no tools except the ability to compartmentalize my feelings and fragment myself. It is no surprise that when I discovered drugs and alcohol at the age of thirteen, it felt like an epiphany. Here was the perfect way to run from myself, to numb my pain, to create what felt like a safe little world all my own where no one could touch me. And even when they did touch me, I couldn't feel it.

Right from the start, I loved using alone. That was my preferred way of getting high, although of course I also did it socially. I would also get high secretly and not tell anyone, sitting there surrounded by people, feeling like a ghost. But what I loved most was sitting in my room by myself, convincing myself that this place I created inside my head was the real world, and the one outside, the one full of people and pain, was just an illusion.

The first time I went to rehab, I was sixteen, driven by a depression that no amount of drugs seemed to improve. I wanted it to work, and I approached sobriety like the straight-A student I was. But after a year and a half, I was lonelier than ever, and I convinced myself that I could drink and use like a normal person. Not even two years later, I dropped out of my dream college, addicted to cocaine, suffering severe mental health issues, and wanting to die.

By the time I finally got sober at age twenty-eight. I had spent years eking out a life despite myself. I hit a few bottoms on my way there, but somehow I ended up with a promising career, a nice partner, and a house. As always, I lived a double life, my troubled inner world hidden by my armor of privilege and accomplishment. But I was so tired. I had tried in vain for years to control my drinking and drug use, doing all the things we do to lie to ourselves. I managed to quit drugs, but I would always drink again, not knowing what else to do with the feelings that would inevitably come up, the discomfort I had no idea how to sit with.

I went to rehab again and threw myself into AA. I was lucky to have gotten sober in the Bay Area, where the 12-step community was diverse and progressive, where it was possible to find a cozy niche of women's and queer meetings that felt like home, where they didn't say the Lord's prayer, and where their approach to the program and the Big Book was more trauma-informed and less dogmatic than many other places.

For the first time in my life, I felt like I found my people, and I began finding myself. I learned how to be close to people. I learned how to take responsibility for my actions, and I learned that my actions affected other people. Somehow, that had never occurred to me. I had been so consumed by my own pain for so much of my life, in some way I had started to believe I was the only one who felt anything.

I had a good early recovery in 12-steps, and I am grateful. In my first few years, I also started exploring Buddhism, going to a day-long retreat and a few meditation groups here and there, reading everything I could find about a Buddhist approach to the 12-steps. I thought I, and my program, were invincible. At five years sober and a mother to an almost one-year old, my partner and I decided we were done with city living and moved across the country to the mountains of North Carolina. I had always been good at moving, running from problem to problem and starting over somewhere else. But this time, I wasn't running from something — or so I thought. My life in the Bay Area had been wonderful, but I was ready to start the next chapter of my life.

Something was missing, and I thought I would find it in this unfamiliar place surrounded by strangers.

But it didn't go quite as planned. I had expected to just fall into 12-steps here and find a new friend group like I did back in California. But the meetings were weird, full of a southern Christian God and what seemed like questionable recovery. The old-timers sounded like cult leaders. The repetition of readings and sayings and slogans began to wear thin. With the stress of a young child and a huge life transition, and without the community we had back in the Bay, the cracks in my marriage also started to show. I was lonely in North Carolina, and the foundation of both my recovery and my personal life was starting to feel shaky.

Then I found a flier on a coffee shop bulletin board for a Buddhist recovery group, and I decided to give it a try. The meeting was just a handful of quirky-looking people sitting on cushions in a circle on the floor, talking about their lives in what felt like a refreshingly intimate and authentic way. I immediately felt like this was the room I wanted to be in.

Over the next several months, I found a home in this new community. I began to see my personal growth with a Buddhist lens, addiction as something much deeper than a dependency on chemicals or even a disease. Yearning was the human condition, and we addicts, through whatever concoction of trauma and adverse childhood experiences and hereditary influences, came to feel these yearnings more intensely, often for things beyond substances. Buddhism deepened my recovery in ways

I never imagined possible in 12-steps, inviting me to not only look outward at systems created by others, but ultimately look inward and trust my own Wisdom.

That is not to say I think I know all the answers. I certainly knew very little about how to live an honest and healthy life when I got sober, and I needed to look outward for wisdom, to trusted groups and people who I knew had something valuable to teach me. I believe being humble is essential to wisdom. But as my recovery deepens, so does my trust of my ability to make healthy choices — and to also know when I need help figuring out what those healthy choices are.

It is easy for me to focus solely on the inward-looking aspects of Buddhism and convince myself sometimes that this is a solitary path. But there is a reason sangha is one of the three jewels at the core of this path, and I know I cannot do this alone.

It is easy for me to make Buddhism complicated, to over-intellectualize, but I also know that I feel most grounded when I focus on just being with experience rather than judging or analyzing it. When in doubt, I remind myself of the core teaching: *do no harm*. I remind myself that includes not doing harm to myself.

Buddhist recovery has taught me the importance of being kind and gentle to myself. It has taught me to look at my intentions and motivations for doing things. It has helped me understand that I can find peace regardless of what is happening outside of myself, and that I do not need external validation to feel that I am enough. And I am finding that the more I feel that I am enough, the less I crave other things to fill me up.

When we started Recovery Dharma, one of our core intentions was to emphasize that this is a program of empowerment, not powerlessness. Acceptance of what is is part of equanimity and integral to our liberation, but that is not the same as powerlessness. As a writer, I know that words matter. As a survivor of trauma among so many other survivors of trauma, I know that powerlessness is not what I want my recovery to be based on. Instead, I see my recovery as a path towards wholeness and embodied, empowered choices.

I may not always have power over what happens in the world, what happens to me, or even my own feelings, but I have power in how I choose to respond. Sometimes that power is limited by old patterns and trauma response, but it is still there. My Buddha nature, my liberation, is always inside me, always accessible. I have the power to be kind and gentle to myself and others. I have the power to set boundaries, and also to forgive. I have the power to look at my various human yearnings and discern what is motivated by craving versus what is motivated by curiosity, connection, and joy. I have the power to be present and breathe through whatever life brings me, and to be grateful for all of it.

CHANCE

Dharma, sobriety, and my identity are delightfully blended.

The pivotal push to getting sober was a feeling of disconnection from my chosen family, and from myself. An occasionally deep, often mild, haunting sensation of hindered intimacy. I wanted to show up and be truly me, meeting truly them, but there was always this cloudy curtain between us.

When I was eleven, I started with alcohol, and my mom was one of those "as long as it's at home, substance use is okay" kind of parents. I was eleven and a lot of my friends were sixteen, so you know we were drinking and driving, and then soon added pot, and acid, and mushrooms. I grew up in rural Ohio, and nature was a big part of my experience as a teen. We talked like we thought the substances brought us closer to nature and its beauty and mystery, but probably we would have gotten closer to the elements had we been sober and actually present. Either way, I was able to escape home and two parents who didn't talk, slept in separate beds, and yet supposedly were staying together for me — by zipping off and flying high with my crew. I also did a lot of drugs with my mom. She introduced me to cocaine, meth, and crack. Our shared dependence was a distorted parent-child closeness. She was, and still is, hurt and lonely.

I excelled in my tiny Catholic high school. I was a perfectionist, took all the advanced classes, skipped a grade in French, wrote for the newspaper, pushed vegetarianism. I eventually graduated as the valedictorian. I'd jam all my homework during lunch time so that I'd be free to check out as fully as possible from after school until bedtime with drugs. And that was the cycle, day after day.

My queerness emerged early on. In 6th grade, I famously declared, "When I grow up, I'm going to be bisexual." Which to this day, I'm fully embodying. However, in small town, sex-negative USA, this was easier said than done. When I became (at that time) a girl kissing girls, the hang ups and harassing phone calls to our house line started happening. I never denied my desires or who I am, and I paid for it, but I never considered another way to be. I had a high school girlfriend when I was in 8th grade, and we partied and learned bodies.

College and grad school were more of the same. Me working so hard and then rewarding myself at the end of the day and fuzzing out. More and more special people came into my life, through queer, activist, and academic communities. I love relationship building, exploring, navigating, co-finding channels for growth and creativity. Yet I felt the channels were blocked, and separation was apparent.

In Fall 2012, I decided my drinking was out of control. I had never really liked alcohol. Both of my parents were alcoholics and addicts, and I just couldn't be like them. So I cut out the alcohol, because I thought that was the problem. Things definitely felt less chaotic, and my body felt better. But the drugs continued - so much marijuana daily, plus MDMA and psychedelics often. The disconnection with my romantic partners was palpable, so I enacted a "sober sex only" policy for myself and my dates. I learned quite a bit about queerness, presence, and substances then. Many people couldn't easily set aside drinks and/or drugs in preparation for sex. These early negotiations around substances and physicality were significant. They were empowering, and I was able to practice directness and consent.

Yet stopping at sober sex wasn't enough. After six months of the policy, the same six months on gender-affirming hormone therapy, I went on a trip to Las Vegas with a sex worker collective I was part of, and — while I didn't know that it would be the last time — I took my last dose of drugs in the desert. The next day was my dad's birthday, not an uncomplicated date, and that became my sobriety anniversary.

I stopped because I had had enough. On that desert walk in my altered state, alone but with others, I just thought about how I could get to so many of these same places with my meditation practice and so much less clinging and opacity. I was in the middle of a 90 and 90 meditation challenge I was doing with a dharma buddy, where we would meditate 90 minutes a day for 90 days. I was committed, and I was ready for change.

Upon abstaining, I had a built-in network of sober friends from my meditation community, which held a lot of sober punks. At the same time, it felt like a magnificent shift and very organic. It was simple, but not easy. I lost friends. I broke up with most of my romantic relationships. A lot of people asking "WHY???" "You don't have a problem?" "You never seemed like things got out of control," etc., etc. This still happens, and I'm celebrating my ten-year soberversary.

Getting sober required a lot of release. Staying sober requires doing all the ancillary work, in addition to being active in a recovery community. Dharma, sangha, honesty, connection, communication, compassion, rupture, repair…this one-line string of words and principles encapsulates an ever-challenging life practice of being a better person and causing less harm and bringing more joy into the world. I'm extremely grateful to be embedded in a community that can reflect back these values while we all stumble trustfully together.

I am one of the stewards of our first NYC-area queer Recovery Dharma meeting, and it's truly magic. Queer and trans people healing together on this path, we especially need each other and this space where we can process shared experience and difficulties. Service has always been a large part of my recovery. Whether I was an Intersangha Rep, or Events Chair organizing daylong retreats and my favorite — the New Year's Eve gathering, meeting chair, mentor/wise friend, meeting location finder and conduit…showing up, opening up, being an anchor, feeling anchored by others, and holding space is central to nourishing the group's collective health and continuation.

I like this saying that I've heard from a few Dharma teachers, "Don't waste your suffering." For me, this points to the power of transformation in the Eightfold Path. It's especially supportive because it's not a consecutive sequence. To me, the Dharma is kaleidoscopic. Each little bit of the path catches and mirrors back countless other pieces of the path.

I've spent a lot of time tuning into ethics (known as sīla in Pāli), the three stages along the Eightfold Path — right speech, right action, and right livelihood. Growing up, I received messages that it was okay to screw other people over to get ahead. This ethos ran deep, and I've had to, and continue to do a lot of undoing and behavioral remodeling work. I don't waste the suffering that can be transmuted when I am tempted to or act in an unskillful way and catch myself. I check how my body and heart feel, note it, and investigate those qualities. I also try not to beat myself up and instead practice self-compassion. And when I choose a skillful action, I feel into the gratitude and joy, how it emerges in my body, and I try to expand that.

A big part of staying sober has also been handling loss. A couple years ago, my ex-partner died from addiction. They weren't only my ex-partner, but they were one of my strongest recovery inspirations when I was in early sobriety. Together we founded the group that would later become Recovery Dharma NYC. I am still taking advice they shared when we were in each other's lives. And I'm heartbroken that the pull of escaping with substances overpowered their ability to take one of their own pieces of advice that they gave me after they started using again, "It's much easier to stay sober than to get sober." They told me they struggled with presenting as trans feminine in the world while sober — the frequent affronts of harassment, rage, rudeness, and microaggressions were heavy to handle.

As a trans (masculine) person, I have experienced much of this myself, and I know that transphobia is amplified against trans feminine people. I'm also grateful that myself and many other trans and gender diverse people have found continued strength and clarity in sobriety and support from our practices and networks to keep going.

"I love you, keep going." This is a metta phrase that was passed down from a Dharma teacher years back, one that appears often in my reflections. I, like all beings, am deserving of love, including my own love. It all starts there. I will persist and resist the narratives and attacks against trans people. Especially in this time when there is an intensely targeted political attack on our existence.

I am training to face reality, and to see it for what it is. Here are some snapshots of my practice. Everyday, I sit down to meditate. Maybe it's 45 minutes, or 5 minutes, or somewhere in between. I heard a teacher once say that even just paying attention to 1 breath counts. After I meditate, I recite the Five Remembrances, or listen to monks chanting them in a video online:

> I am of the nature to grow old, there is no escaping growing old. I am of the nature to get sick, there is no escaping sickness. I am of the nature to die, there is no escaping death. Everyone and everything I love are of the nature to change, and there is no escaping separation from them. My actions are my only belongings, I cannot escape their consequences, they are the ground upon which I stand.

Next I recite one round of classic metta phrases. I close my sit with taking refuge in the Buddha, Dharma, and Sangha.

I build on my daily sitting and life practice with residential practice periods. I do at least one 7-10 day silent meditation retreat per year (this year I did my first metta retreat, and it was incredibly fruitful), plus spend a week at a Thai Forest Buddhist Monastery. I'm grateful for the opportunities for these extended, dedicated practice periods, and believe that they have contributed immensely to expanding and strengthening wisdom, balance, and heartfulness.

I'm still continuing to identify impermanence (*anicca*), ungovernability (*anatta*), and unsatisfactoriness (*dukkha*) and the ways in which I relate to them, and I don't doubt that these will be lifelong tasks. But I'm seeing them a lot more, and clearer, and this naturally has made recovery more attainable, and intoxication much less desirable. Escaping doesn't lead to lasting happiness, in fact in my experience, it just prolongs and sometimes solidifies whatever I'm trying to get away from. The benefits of being in touch with these three marks of existence are many — increased appreciation and presence, awareness of the vast webs and chains of interdependence, and a letting be of things being what I want and how I want them. Recovery Dharma has kept me rooted and rejoicing.

You can read another iteration of my story in the *Transcending: Trans Buddhist Voices* anthology.

SYNYI
Content Warning: Suicide

I found Recovery Dharma during the lowest and most transformative time of my life. The popsicle sticks and glue that I used to contain my overwhelm and despair came crashing down around me. I'd later learn to refer to these popsicle sticks as substance use and process addictions, and that my overwhelm was rooted in untreated depression and trauma. Looking back on my recovery journey, I am grateful for the experience, learning, and healing, but it was hard-earned.

My story starts in kindergarten, when I immigrated with my parents. Overnight, my world changed — a foreign place with a new language, knowing almost no one, a new school where I couldn't understand anybody, and my parents working all the time to survive. They did their best, but an asleep parent isn't a present parent, and I had to learn independence from a young age.

I grew up seeing my parents model working hard, sacrificing their needs, acting strong, and never talking about feelings. I learned that my role in the family was to study hard, to not be a burden with my needs, push down my feelings, and that I needed to be happy so that their sacrifices were worth it.

By high school, I'd been pushing down fears and insecurities for years. I was doing well in school, and that came with some self-worth and external validation, but I also felt so alone. The closer friendships I'd developed were always cut short by one of us moving away. So I entered high school with no real friends but luckily got adopted by an extrovert who I shared a geography class with.

Finding some friends slowly built some confidence, but even in that circle, I felt like I was on the periphery, overthinking and worrying that I wasn't good enough, attractive enough, cool enough to have friends. But I got by, pushing down those insecurities. Later in high school, I found myself with people who had access to weed, and when I smoked, the incessant chatter in my mind cleared. I could be in on the secret and didn't have to worry about being uncool for once because everything was just hilarious instead.

But when I was living my usual sober life as a straight-laced nerd, I was fraught with social anxiety and low self-esteem. The next times of my life were fueled by fear and external validation. I started to gain the external markers of success: I graduated top of my class, attracted romantic partners, got a coveted job, moved into a condo in the city. On the outside, things were great, but inside I was frightened constantly that the perfect facade would crack and everyone would see me as a fraud. I fell into coping mechanisms: working constantly and seeking perfection because if I was perfect then the fear of not being "good enough" felt a little less intense.

On evenings to "treat myself" for the shitty life I put up with, I'd smoke weed from the moment I walked through the door until I eventually passed out in a smoke-filled oblivion, and every weekend was wake and bake. I was living only for the weekends, going to raves and festivals, taking party drugs and chasing the serotonin highs and feelings of connectedness that made me feel something other than the depression and anxiety that plagued my workdays. I started going to work high and my roommates and close friends started to tell me that they were worried about me. Honestly I was worried about me too.

During a particularly stressful time at work, I went on vacation and came home wondering why I was staying in a job I hated. I'm fortunate that I had saved up some money, and so I quit without a job lined up and decided I was going to travel. Surely my location was the problem and if I traveled to beautiful destinations, then I would be happy. I was leaving on a trip to try to outrun my anxiety and depression, and maybe find some key to happiness because other solutions to stress, like mindfulness, hadn't worked for me.

I now understand that with the unresolved trauma, my mind was a place that lacked self-compassion and my body felt unsafe when I sat still. It felt like such serendipity when I was struck by the idea that some people turn to religion in times of uncertainty and fear, so my desperation turned me to giving my parent's Buddhist religion a try. Up to this point, I had been an adamant atheist, though I always obeyed when my parents wanted me to go with them to the nearby Buddhist temple.

I didn't understand why we lit incense, bowed three times in front of statues of deities I didn't recognize, and prayed with offerings for good things or for bad things not to happen. It all just seemed like illogical superstition to me. Now that I opened my mind to the idea of Buddhism, I learned about the Theravada and Mahayana traditions in Southeast Asia, and they spoke to me so much more than my parents' practices. I searched online for a beginner intro to Buddhism and found Jetsunma Tenzin Palmo's book "Into the Heart of Life" and serendipitously again, her preface felt like it spoke directly to me as I was preparing for my trip. I highlighted a passage about how the mind is always with us, with its thoughts and fears from which we can never escape and so it makes sense to try and work with our mind so that it becomes a friendly travel companion for our journey through life.

I dove into the book and became aware of the truth of impermanence and the truth of suffering. It resonated with me so deeply that the Buddha never demanded people to blindly follow his teachings, but instead encouraged them to observe for themselves and see that what he taught was true. And while impermanence and suffering made sense, I couldn't wrap my head around non-attachment or no-self, so I was determined to learn about it on my trip. That's how I ended up volunteering in Thailand, though I can't say I learned too much about these Buddhist concepts in Thailand because of the language barrier. However, I did meet some incredibly kind monks and laypeople.

It was true though that no matter how far I went, my mind was always with me. It was telling me that I'm not good enough, that I'm weak since I burned out, and that I'm a broken depressed person who will never be happy if I couldn't even be perfectly happy while seeing these beautiful sights. I'm really glad to say that I have a much healthier relationship with my thoughts and emotions today with the help of lots of therapy, my recovery and Recovery Dharma, and my growing meditation practice.

I eventually grew homesick and came home. I found a corporate job and started living with my now-spouse. We abused weed together every day, and as my job got more stressful, my weed use increased. When the COVID-19 pandemic hit, I was a shell of a person, reclused into myself by overwhelm at work and even more overwhelm by basic things like going to the grocery store.

I would later come to realize that the drastic shift in the world overnight as well as the panic about the unknown was emotionally triggering my trauma around immigrating at such a young age. I think I experienced emotional flashbacks of my terror and reverted to my kindergarten psychological capacity. Except this time, I had weed to abuse to try to quell the overwhelming panic. And it worked for a while, until it didn't anymore. I started down into the worst episode of depression I ever experienced — I lost interest in friends, hobbies, and my partner, and I shut down. It was really scary when I lost the ability to concentrate and my work performance declined, especially scary as someone whose self-worth came from work. As my overwhelm and terror grew, I turned to weed during the work day too and I hated myself for it. I entered a cycle of panic, using, feeling a few minutes of relief, and then hating myself for being weak for giving in to the craving.

The height of my addiction, or my metaphorical bottom, came when I lost the will to live. My attempt on my life luckily ended with me in the emergency room. I was admitted to inpatient treatment and detoxed from marijuana while attending group therapy and learned the powerful feeling of connection when someone says "me too." I had started therapy about a year before, but because I was high all the time, I wasn't mindful of my thoughts and feelings outside of therapy sessions, so progress was slow. I left inpatient treatment with a waiting list spot for an outpatient program, a recommendation that I give up marijuana and attend psychologist follow-up sessions. I remember being told that depression was a three-pronged combination of bio, psycho, social, and that I would need to address bio with medication, psycho with therapy, and social by building up a mental well-being support system.

For social support, I found my way to the rooms of Marijuana Anonymous where I heard other people telling stories that were similar to mine and it really helped me to stay off the weed. But the "singleness of purpose" tradition in 12-Step felt stifling because my problem wasn't only marijuana use, it was also the trauma I was unearthing in the "psycho" prong. Again I come back to serendipity. The Recovery Dharma program was exactly what I needed at the time. I received a suggestion to attend a second recovery meeting on a day that I had already been to an MA meeting, and curious, I went searching for alternatives.

Through the Buddhist Recovery Network website, I found Recovery Dharma. When I visited the website, I was delighted to find that the Recovery Dharma book was readily available for free on the website, that it was accessible to me in my time of need. I devoured the book quickly — it helped me to frame my addiction in the teachings of the Buddha that I had already developed an interest in. Now revisiting the Dharma with my new lived experience of addiction, the truth of suffering took on new meaning.

I found a sangha that met almost daily. And almost every day, I came and sat in meditation with like-minded travelers on the path. We could talk about anything, without the restrictions of "singleness of purpose." It was exactly what I needed because it helped me learn to meditate with the safety of a group, and I learned the language of talking about my trauma from reading the trauma-informed RD book, listening to shares, and practicing during my own shares.

Today I feel like I'm thriving, not merely surviving. I've been sober from my "drug of no choice" for almost 3 years, and I've made great progress managing my process addictions of workaholism and perfectionism. I'm practicing real self love, gratitude, meditation, and validating my own feelings. My family, friends, and work are all going better than ever before. I can be present for my loved ones. I am able to take care of my darling cat and accept her love. I'm able to give back by hosting meetings in service of my sangha. I'm also blessed to be able to volunteer my professional skills as an RD Global Board Member and serve on Board committees.

I have cultivated an understanding of myself, my trauma, triggers and coping mechanisms, so that I can weather the emotional storms when they come and give myself loving-kindness. There is hope and joy in my life, as well as strength and security in knowing that although I can't carpet the whole world, I can put on shoes as I continue my travels, with my healthier mind and spirit as my companion.

MATTHEW
Content Warning: Suicide

One December morning, I made myself a cup of Folgers coffee and peered out the bars of my prison cell. My cellmate had gone to the yard and I had some time alone. Watching an armed guard walk past on the catwalk outside, I pondered life.

"Why didn't anybody tell me it would hurt this much?" I asked myself. I was twenty-seven years old, recently sober, and barely two years into a fourteen year prison sentence. Things were actually getting better, though it was hard to see at the time.

It hadn't always hurt that much. It had started out as fun.

Growing up, there was always a case of cheap beer inside the fridge in the garage. It was there mostly for guests since neither of my parents really drank. I was eight years old the first time I stole one of those beers and drank it in the backyard. It was cold and crisp and left my tiny body feeling quite wonderful. I would remember it later.

I was part of the "Just Say No" generation. My youth was filled with memories of DARE (Drug Abuse Resistance Education) classes, Nancy Reagan admonishments against drug use, and commercials with eggs crackling in a frying pan. I had ideas about what my brain would do on drugs.

I was a curious kid with a natural distrust of authority. When I was told not to do something, I tended toward trying it at least once. Just to be sure. My attitude toward drugs was no different.

At twelve, I tried weed. I'd stolen it from a babysitter and smoked it from a pipe made of tin foil. When none of the terrifying things that were promised me in DARE classes developed, I came to the erroneous conclusion that my parents, teachers, and First Lady had all been lying to me about drugs. Within short order, I was smoking pot with other latchkey kids, spending the hours after school and before our parents came home experimenting with our new form of entertainment. It was actually just fun.

At thirteen years old, the fun started to subside. I was arrested at a school dance for possession of marijuana and was suspended for a week. I had always been a good kid and a good student. I'd never been in any serious trouble at school. This was a first for me.

When I returned to school after my suspension, I swiftly realized that people treated me differently. I got attention from kids that normally wouldn't have paid me any mind. Teachers started treating me like an adult. I'd always been smart but too rough around the edges for the nerdy kids, and I'd always been too nerdy for the jockish crowd. Suddenly, I'd found a role that fit me: the smart kid with a wild streak. If the role didn't fit me well at first, I made sure that I fit myself into it.

High school was a bit of blur. Drug and alcohol use that started out as recreational transformed into daily ritual. Booze and weed eventually included hallucinogens. Cocaine and crank were added to the cocktail. Finally, I found crystal methamphetamine.

I did meth for the first time during my senior year of high school. Something was different about this drug. I felt invincible, I felt like a god. I became a near-daily meth user from the start. Meth became a swift wrecking ball in my life. Within three months of use, I had dropped out of high school and was stealing as a way to support my habit.

When I first started stealing, I tried to have some semblance of ethics about it, ridiculous as that sounds. I didn't steal from individuals. I didn't steal from cars. I didn't steal from homes. But my willingness to cross boundaries with stealing followed a similar progression as my willingness to try increasingly harder drugs, and I eventually found myself stealing whatever I could get my hands on. At eighteen, I was arrested for a string of burglaries and sentenced to more than five years in prison. I paroled at the legal age for drinking.

During my time in county jail, in prison, and on parole, I was introduced to recovery. Twice, I stayed in 30-day residential treatment facilities and was exposed to 12-step programs. I went to meetings and superficially did what was asked of me. Even though it looked like I was in recovery, I wasn't actually doing recovery. My goal was not to stay sober but was, instead, to look good for parents, judges, and parole agents. Though I had decided that I would never use hard drugs like meth again, I had no designs on staying completely sober. I wanted to drink and smoke pot when life circumstances would allow for it.

I started drinking again while I was on parole and, as soon as my state supervision ended, I resumed smoking pot. I used "successfully" like this for a couple of years. I was going to college and doing well. I had a great job. Relationships with family were mostly restored. I had nothing to be concerned about.

Around this time, I took an Eastern Philosophy course in college and was introduced to the teachings of the Buddha. I read about the Four Noble Truths and the three characteristics of existence and felt a great sense of familiarity with them, like they represented a truth that I'd known all along but had somehow forgotten. I just knew the Dharma to be true but, at the same time, I decided that I wasn't suffering enough to worry about it just yet. I would get my chance.

A couple of years after leaving prison, one of my closest childhood friends committed suicide in a very violent manner. It was the closest death had come in my life thus far and it shook me. I felt like the world was crumbling in on me, that I'd been emotionally and spiritually shaken from a foundation. I didn't know how to cope with the way I felt and I didn't have the inner resources to ask for help. I became a daily drinker and relapsed on methamphetamine a few months later.

I started stealing again and my life snowballed in the same way it had seven years earlier. Overwhelmed with sadness, beset with remorse for the harm I was causing yet again, and burdened with shame at the thought of seeking help, I considered suicide but got loaded instead. An imperfect solution, the drugs saved me from myself.

Yet again, I was arrested for a string of burglaries. I found myself facing centuries in prison under California's three strikes law. In the county jail and without the option of getting loaded, my suffering was inescapable. My sadness was inescapable. My remorse was inescapable. My shame, my suicidal ideation, everything, was inescapable. I was forced to look everything square in the face.

There's a reason that the First Noble Truth is about suffering. No transformative path begins without it. Convinced that my life couldn't possibly get any worse than it was at the moment, I decided upon two things. First, I would try my hand at recovery. The worst thing that could happen was nothing. Second, recalling the Buddhism I'd encountered in college three years earlier, I'd give meditation and the Dharma a try.

That was in 2005. There was no mindfulness or Buddhist-based recovery available, so finding recovery and following the Dharma started out as separate paths. On one hand, I started going to 12-step meetings in the county jail, found a sponsor on the streets, and began the process of writing inventories and making amends. On the other hand, I started meditating as best as I knew how. Without a teacher, the internet, or a sangha, I relied solely upon the books that family would generously send me.

I completely misused meditation when I first started practice. Instead of using meditation as a method for meeting reality, I used it as an escape. In this way, meditation served as a substitute for the drugs I no longer had easy access to. I do not judge myself for using my practice this way in the beginning; in so many ways, it was exactly what I needed at the time. I would eventually develop the skills to face my reality more squarely, but it would take time.

After a year and half in the county jail, I accepted a plea bargain of fourteen years in prison. By the time I arrived in Folsom State Prison later that year, I'd been clean from drugs and alcohol for nearly two years, I was prepared to start mentoring other incarcerated men in recovery, and my meditation practice was becoming consistent.

At Folsom, I finally sat in meditation with other people. Two nights per week, I met with Sangha in the fabled Greystone Chapel. Facilitated by volunteers from the outside, these groups were where I really came to understand what mindfulness practice was about. I finally had fellows on the path, and I finally had teachers. Both were absolutely necessary to the flourishing of my meditation and Dharma practice.

Every afternoon during count, loud buzzers would sound off in the cell block. So, every afternoon, half an hour before count time, I rolled up a blanket and sat on the floor of my cell. The prison would be my timer. My meditation changed dramatically. No longer was it a method of escape; instead, it became a method inquiry. In the beginning, it was simple. What was it like to breathe? What was it like to sit on my rolled-up blanket? What was the nature of the sounds in my cell block?

With practice, I started to see that the present moment wasn't as bad as I thought it was. In fact, the present moment, when I wasn't actually thinking about it, was mostly neutral and oftentimes pleasant. This was a bit of a breakthrough for me, because some part of me was convinced that I was supposed to be miserable in prison.

Yes, being in prison was awful. Yes, being away from friends and family was awful. Yes, washing my clothes in the toilet was awful. Yes, yes, yes. But, in time, I came to realize that these things were only awful insofar as I found myself mesmerized by my own narratives about them. My stories about my life were the problem, and I had a lot of them.

Prison, I could not escape. There was no freedom from prison while I was living there. There was, however, freedom from my story about it. I did not have to take prison personally. This insight carried me through the remainder of my prison sentence and into the outside world.

I paroled after seven years of incarceration. There was still no mindfulness or Buddhist-based recovery, so I continued to do in the free world what I had done inside: attend recovery meetings and meditation groups separately. Though I was immensely grateful for the recovery program I had, I nonetheless translated a great deal of the 12-step program into Buddhist terms and practices which better aligned with the way I moved through the world. Finally, after ten years of renunciation from drugs and alcohol, a Buddhist-based path of recovery was developed and I helped to establish it in my local area. This program eventually became the Recovery Dharma of today. I no longer needed to translate my program of recovery.

Since coming home, I have found that six things have been integral to my continued growth in recovery and as a human being. Meditation. Meetings. Study. Service. Friends. Teachers.

I meditate every day and try to participate in a minimum of two silent retreats every year. I regularly attend recovery meetings and other Buddhist meditation groups. I study the teachings of the Buddha in order to develop a deeper understanding of ways to implement them in my life. I take on service positions in my Recovery Dharma groups and share the message of recovery and of the Dharma wherever I can. I maintain friendships with people who nurture and support my own growth. I regularly meet with both a mentor and a Buddhist teacher in order to navigate difficulties in practice and continue to move forward on the path.

My life has been both challenging and beautiful since coming home from prison more than a decade ago.

I have completed state supervision and graduated from university. I have completed a five-year trade apprenticeship and become an elected union official. I have gotten married to a wonderful woman in recovery and become a homeowner. I've traveled to Buddhist pilgrimage sites in India and participated in extended meditation retreats at home and abroad. I have received lay ordination within a Buddhist tradition and started teaching the Dharma to people in California prisons.

I have also navigated complex PTSD and started to unlearn prison survival strategies that were no longer useful to me. I have been present for death when it sweeps through and survived life-altering heart surgery.

Mindfulness, heartfulness, and community are what made and continue to make all of these possible. As one of my teachers has said, Dharma practice has the capacity to transform the very nature of suffering. Awakening might not come in the form of sudden moments of revelation, but instead may entail the gradual digestion of pain and trauma. Over the years, I have progressively come to see the good that has come from past suffering and I try my best to carry that perceptive in the present moment, reshaping it with wisdom and love. One line from Recovery

Dharma's dedication of merit stands out to me: "As we have learned from practice, great pain does not erase goodness, but in fact informs it." This isn't just a platitude. It's a promise.

BERLINDA
Content Warning: Childhood sex abuse

My story shows how a person can go from real hardship to a life of balance using community, prayer, the Four Noble Truths and the Eightfold Path. Trauma made me want to numb myself with substances and my practice has allowed me to feel those feelings from the past without reaching out to something to harm myself further.

My childhood was pretty rough. I was raised by a woman who was a sex worker and when I turned eleven years old, she started to traffic me as well. I learned to leave my body and disassociate because that was the only way I could deal with it. I lived that way for a long time. My mother didn't allow us to play with other children of color. We would get beatings for that even though she was dark; a "Morena" herself. Eventually, I was placed in a children's mental institution because I stopped talking. I was there for a couple years before they sent me back to my mother.

When I got home, one of my abusers was visiting my mother so I ran away the first day I came back. As soon as I saw him at the top of the steps, I took off. There was a local delivery boy who I liked and he let me hang out at his apartment while he was working. I told him I didn't want to go back home and about what was going on there. He told me that when he came back from work he would have something for me and that ended up being a bottle. I took that first drink and it felt like, my God, where have you been. Everything disappeared from my mind. I just wanted to have fun. I was giggly for the first time in a very long time.

I had stopped going to school during the third grade. There were no social services at the time; at least for my neighborhood. You didn't see them unless the school complained. I was in and out of juvenile detention and one female lawyer told me I was inappropriately dressed for court and gave me her own stockings to wear for the proceedings. I wanted to stay with her because she was nice to me.

At fifteen, I was emancipated from my mother and began working at a bar. This older lady I met on the bus asked me if I wanted to work. I thought it was going to be cleaning houses or something but when I asked her what she wanted me to do she told me about the bar. The first day I went in for the interview, I had never been inside a bar before and they were putting all these shot glasses in front of me and I asked the lady, Miss. Mary, what the shot glasses were for. She told me eagerly that men were buying me drinks. Since I didn't like the taste of alcohol, she taught me how to make a lemon drop chaser with a slice of lemon covered in sugar. I got hooked on those. I drank for the sensation. I got myself ready for drinks, it was a treat. This was in 1970 at the Golden Slipper on Webster Avenue in the Bronx.

Eventually I found out the go-go dancers at the bar made a lot more money than I did, so I started doing that. I liked it because I didn't actually have to get involved with the men, it was all an illusion. I go-go danced for nine years and made a lot of money. I worked long hours at different places around the city and I drank through all of it. I didn't know that I had crossed that invisible line of addiction. I would isolate and drink, I didn't want to share my drink, I would get territorial with my alcohol. I would keep cups of alcohol around my apartment in different rooms, one in the bathroom next to the toothbrush, one next to the bed which I would reach for as soon as I woke up in the morning.

I gave birth to my daughter when I was almost eighteen. My mother took her because it was either sign her over to my mother or release her to the system. I didn't raise her myself because I couldn't stay with my mother, and I thought that at least I could still see her if she's with family.

I met my husband in the neighborhood. We went to a party together and he came home with me and never left. When I met him he was sniffing heroin and drinking but I made him stop the heroin. He said if I stopped dancing he would marry me the next year. We had a son and, when he was three, my husband wanted us to move to Virginia because his family was down there. We both got jobs, he did maintenance, I cleaned houses. He started getting abusive to the point where I would check into a psych ward for the weekend just to get away from him for a while. I applied for a job at the Department of Corrections (DOC) and he hid the acceptance letter from me under the mattress. He didn't want me making more money because he wouldn't have as much control over me.

In May 1990, I received my first paycheck from the DOC, and I got my own apartment. I put up bunk beds and gave my son the bedroom while I slept out in the living room on a daybed.

During my second or third year at the DOC, I went to a party with fellow officers and they had a lot of coke, so me and another girl went into the kitchen and started cooking it. At the time it was called "freebasing". Before I left the party that night, I was addicted. I ultimately stopped using crack because of my son. I went to my Major and told her I had a problem, and they sent me to rehab.

I was sober for a long time until I met Keena working a temp job at Great Adventure. We figured out a scam where we could pocket ticket money directly, and one day we made $1,500 each. Keena wanted to score drugs with the money, and I told her I would have just a little bit, but we were up all night long. That's when it started up again. We moved up to New Jersey together with my son because he had gotten kicked out of high school in Virginia. He didn't want me to be with Keena, and so he moved out, which hurt me. He felt like I picked her over him, but I felt like my personal relationships were none of his business.

I started having feelings for women when I started dancing but I didn't take it seriously until later. My son knew that I was gay. I had met another woman previously and we were "married"; it's not like it is today, so we had what was called a "holy union". The ceremony took place at a gay church and the pastor asked us what colors we were using in our wedding and we told him purple and silver. He wore purple and silver vestments for our ceremony. She was always good to me. Even after we broke up she helped me raise my son, and they're still in touch to this day. She helped me pay rent and got me a new truck, but all that stopped once Keena came into my life.

Keena and I would argue over who did more of the drugs. I tried to solve our problems by moving, but as soon as we set foot in our new town she was out looking for drugs again. I found a job working for an elderly lady, and she had two large pickle jars full of quarters at her home, and Keena went in there and stole all that lady's money. And of course *I* got fired. One day when Keena didn't come home, I called Catholic Charities and they put me in a hotel and got me a ticket out of there. Something told me to not look back or say goodbye or nothing. I was so concerned with getting away from her I didn't notice the days and months of sobriety stacking up.

Eventually I came back to New York and started hanging out with the wrong people and picked up crack again; it was something familiar. I lost my apartment and found myself living in an abandoned building with a bunch of other drug users. I moved to a shelter which is where I attended my first 12-step meeting. I went to so many meetings that the facilitator told me I was ready for a meeting outside the shelter. It was on Broadway between 106th and 107th street.

That became my home group and the shelter found me an apartment and I moved back to the Bronx. 12-step showed me that I was my own worst enemy and that the only reason I am where I am today is for the grace of God. He was my rehab, for real. He keeps it simple for me.

It still felt like I needed something else; like something was missing. I was surfing the net one day during the height of the 2020 pandemic and I found Recovery Dharma and went to an online meeting. The spirituality of it was very attractive to me. Even though I was new to this type of fellowship, when people spoke I really identified with what they were saying. I asked about a sponsor, or in this case, a mentor, and they hooked me up with another woman who was also living in the Bronx.

I feel safe to tell my whole story in RD because its consideration of people's trauma is part of the practice. I've gone to quite a few different RD meetings and they all have had the same calm energy, I think of it as Buddha energy. There can be tears in meetings and there's no shame. RD is a safe space and I needed that type of energy in my life. 12-steps was the opening, but now there are different and deeper dimensions of recovery, and RD did that for me.

One thing our practice has helped me with is my reactivity. Because of my daily meditation practice and the teachings of the Four Noble Truths and Eightfold Path, I can take a pause before reacting to something that makes me angry. I am still a work in progress, but I know that I'm not in the street anymore and I don't have to protect myself like that. The wise one says to listen and be still. I know I'm getting better because someone said something unwise to me the other day, and I didn't say anything, I just gave them a look over my glasses.

Recovery Dharma has helped me have compassion for myself and others. This has helped me receive love and care from other people, something I haven't been used to. While I don't live the Four Noble Truths and the Eightfold Path perfectly, I strive to. I pray for that. I meditate every morning with a wise friend and lately I've been using healing meditations because I have chronic pain and it's been helpful.

Please don't let me leave you with the impression that this practice is easy because it's not. I used to avoid feeling and now I feel everything. I've learned that when stuff comes up I just let it play out. Sometimes you need to just let the record play. I have a record that was chiseled into my body and there's nothing I can do about that but I try and catch the feelings so I can identify if they're from past or present, if it's guilt or shame. When my past pain haunts me I stop and breath slowly and chant my favorite mantra: *Om tare tuttare ture soha.*

JEAN

I started drinking at age eight and within a few years, I was an expert on French wines.

My father had died in a plane crash when I was four, I'd recovered from a serious bout of spinal meningitis that same year (leaving me with lifelong learning disabilities), and my mom acquired a female lover when I was six. So, really, why not turn to drinking? My drinking accelerated my senior year in high school, which became one long alcoholic blur. I was accepted to college in October of that year, so not a lot was required of me other than to be upright from time to time. My attraction to other girls was starting to emerge, and I drank in part to fit in, but mostly to numb those feelings.

College took me to the University of Colorado-Boulder in 1969. Please feel free to close your eyes and imagine just how crazy that time was. Pure LSD, incredible leaf, psilocybin, 3.2 beer — we had it all plus a healthy dose of campus revolution. I'd gone from high school in a small town in New Hampshire to an epicenter of the zeitgeist. I was completely unprepared and found an immediate escape in drugs and alcohol. My grades suffered and eventually I dropped out. I did finally own my sexuality and found a short-lived romantic relationship that set the stage for the series of loving, albeit disastrous relationships to come.

At 26, I left behind an epically poor performance as a teacher of kids with developmental disabilities and headed to Arcosanti, a visionary architectural and environmental project emerging in the Arizona desert. Armed with an unemployment paycheck from the state of Illinois and no construction skills whatsoever, I became a dishwasher, rebar manager, electrician, bronze foundry worker, and community networker. In my spare time, I was (of course) a village bartender and drug supplier. At Arcosanti, I found both my purpose and my people. We were a bunch of misfits and idealists, a clown car come to life on a daily basis.

My partner at the time and I left Arcosanti in 1980 with everything we owned in our VW Bug. We landed in Cambridge, Massachusetts and started focusing on work and school. I became a daily blackout drinker, sexually promiscuous and emotionally abusive. I hated myself and I still didn't stop. Finally, the relationship ended and my former partner stopped any form of communication with me for 13 years. I had earned every one of those years.

My last drink was Nyquil on July 4, 1986. Or at least I think it was 1986. It's been a while. But I'm sure it was July 4th, I was lonely, in somebody else's house and looking for some kind of relief from anything at all. I'd been to a few 12-step meetings but thoroughly resisted the idea that I belonged with people who couldn't handle their drinking. That just seemed ridiculous to me, and evidence of a complete failure of will.

But I woke up on July 5th and took in the reality that I'd been reduced to someone who drank Nyquil to get high. At that moment, I lost any interest in drinking again and it never came back. I'd lost almost everything: my partner, my home, my self-respect. I literally had no options but to start building a sense of self and doing the work to begin living with integrity, self-respect, and care.

I trundled along with the 12-steps for many years. I did all the stuff — 90 meetings in 90 days, sponsors, social life built around people I'd met in Alcoholics Anonymous, learning to make really bad coffee in church basements, and turning my life over to, well, what? My standing 12-step joke is that I never drank again because I didn't have the energy to get sober again. I tried everything to get my mind around the idea of a higher power, whether that meant the group, the table, or some other random object.

One night, seven years into all of this, I was at a meeting and someone from out of town dropped in. She started talking about the spirit within and the concept of being spirited — honoring and cherishing that quality of spiritedness. I never saw her again, but that night I quit pondering the meaning of higher power and started owning my spiritedness. From that day forward, I became a person in recovery.

It took a few more years to conduct "a searching and fearless moral inventory" because language like that makes me want to hide under the bed, not actually do anything self-reflective. But one afternoon while treading water in a pool in Bethesda, Maryland, I downloaded all my sins to a very nice woman who was serving as my sponsor and she let me know that I'd "got off easy." My track record didn't feel easy to me, but her saying that in such a kind and generous way gave me the emotional space to keep going in recovery.

This same sponsor encouraged me to get inpatient treatment for the history of alcoholism in my family (I'm a third-generation alcoholic). I spent a week at a facility that uses psychodrama and other intense group-oriented therapeutic tools to dig into the mess that was my family and get an understanding of how to end the destructive patterns I had absorbed as a child. I left there feeling free for the first time in my life. Not surprisingly, it was during this period, at about 12 years sober, that I met the woman, Anna, who I'd go on to marry and live with for 24 years.

Several years into our relationship, Anna and I started looking for meditation teachers. We spent numerous weekends at Breitenbush, our local retreat center in the Oregon Cascades, field-testing various specimens. Some of them were boring, some authentically annoying, and some bordering on creepy. I'd seen Noah Levine's profile in the Breitenbush brochure for several years; he looked a little dangerous but interesting so we signed up for a week with him one summer. Within an hour of listening to him, Anna and I looked at each other and knew we'd found our teacher. Noah's practice community was based in Los Angeles, with Against The Stream serving as his hub organization.

I embraced Dharma with a vengeance. I did retreats, listened to endless podcasts by Theravadan teachers such as John Peacock, Christina Feldman, Gil Fronsdal and others. Noah offered a yearlong book study course co-taught by Mathew Brensilver and so we made the quarterly trek to Los Angeles. I went to Noah's Against the Stream events and loved both the practice and the community. I was initially not excited about Refuge Recovery, the Buddhist-adjacent recovery program Noah developed with community members from Against The Stream, but eventually came around to the idea of a Buddhist-based program that flipped the disease model of alcoholism on its tiny little head. Refuge Recovery annual conferences were a celebration of resilience and hope. The community was thriving and, a couple of years in, I took over from Dave Smith as Executive Director. 12-Step saved my life, Dharma study and practice gave me a life worth living.

I'd heard Noah say that "sooner or later you will lose everything" but I didn't think it would ever apply to Against the Stream. But that's exactly what happened. Things fell apart and some handled it skillfully, and some did not. Along with Amy, Dirk, Dan, Don, Gary, Jessica, Matthew, and Paul (and countless others), we started building Recovery Dharma. We wanted to be intentional in our framework — it had to be peer-led and trauma-informed. It had to have a book that was driven by Dharma. A volunteer from Austin put together a website for us in a week. We were intense and focused and more than a little obsessed. Even though the reality of the need for Recovery Dharma came at much personal loss for some of us, building Recovery Dharma was almost always pure joy and a whole lot of anarchy. I'll never forget the day Paul went live with the Facebook page; he was in Vermont and I was in Oregon and we were texting each other nonstop as the numbers grew. Recovery Dharma was driven by love, not always perfect but always steadfast. I am humbled to witness the growth of our program and all of the people who have put so much faith and care into it. We now have over 10,000 people in our main Facebook group and new folks are stepping in every day to be of service. RD has grown from the same five people doing everything to the point that I don't know half the Board nor most of our Facebook administrators. It's incredibly gratifying to see our program unfold in such an authentic and inspiring way.

At 36 or so years into recovery, I continue to enjoy the benefits of the Three Jewels — Buddha, Dharma and Sangha. Dharma teachings and sangha have enabled me to look at each day as an opportunity to live with intention and compassion. I've experienced the 10,000 joys and the 10,000 sorrows in recovery, and Dharma practice has helped me navigate it all with some measure of self-compassion and equanimity. Impermanence is a part of life and the work I've done has enabled me to navigate it while acknowledging the suffering it can bring. I'm at Arcosanti as I write this, wind bells and birds everywhere. I'm not sure what life is going to bring next but I feel hopeful that Dharma study and practice will give me the "strong back and soft front" taught by Zen Buddhist Roshi Joan Halifax. Recovery is for the fearless amongst us who are equally willing to explore the tenderness and vulnerability of the human experience. Experiencing recovery in community has given me a sense of wholeness and love that I couldn't have found on my own. I am indebted to all who share their practice and gifts in our sangha.

DESTINY

My brain has blocked out a lot of memories from early childhood. I suppose this repression is some sort of self-defense mechanism. What I do remember is feeling isolated. I never really had much emotional support. For most of my life, my mom has struggled with drug addiction and my dad has been in prison. My mom and I lived with my grandparents in a small town in the middle of nowhere. It was a home riddled with dysfunction and codependency. Because I lacked understanding of the world and coping skills, I thought I was inadequate and incapable of dealing with life. I remember feeling forgotten, overlooked, alone, and scared.

The town we lived in was predominantly Caucasian and partially racist. I am biracial and I struggled to fit in the small country town. I felt like I was too Black for the white kids and too white for the Black kids. I was also very creative, diverse, and a little eccentric. All the other kids in my school had little cliques, but I never felt genuinely included. By 6th grade, I was self-harming to feel "in-control" of my pain. After having an emotional episode in late middle school, I was prescribed Xanax for a short period. For the first time in my life, I felt like I could disconnect from my harsh reality and relax in my own skin. After the doctor cut me off, I continually found other ways to get Xanax.

In high school, I became friends with another attractive outcast who liked to use pills, marijuana, and alcohol just as much as me. She was my partner in crime. For once, I felt seen and understood. I also started getting into toxic relationships as I searched for love, attention, and affection in all the wrong places. Even though I got good grades, I skipped so much school that I had to drop out; I got my GED shortly after. After turning 19, I went to a strip club where I found myself inspired by a dancer and infatuated with the lifestyle. Being an exotic dancer was like being a comedian, therapist, and actress simultaneously. My regulars loved me because I would listen deeply to them.

At the same time, my intentions were insincere. I only listened to them with the condition of being paid for my time. For the most part, the relationships with my customers were artificial and developed through manipulation. But ultimately the person I hurt the most was myself. I was getting deeper and deeper into my drug addiction. I was also addicted to the fast-paced lifestyle and external validation. I was modeling too, and I became attached to the idea I was only worthy if I was desired by others. I was also in a very long and unhealthy relationship with a person who abused me physically and emotionally.

Eventually, I went to jail a couple times for possession. One time was on the 4th of July. I remember watching the fireworks in the county jail through a tiny window behind the bars of my cell. "How ironic," I thought to myself. Later that night, I started going through withdrawals. In the holding cell, another inmate told me that I was an addict and needed to get help. As my mind spun out and my body shut down, it honestly never occurred to me that she might be right.

When my abusive relationship ended, I spiraled deeper into addiction. To avoid feeling alone and unwanted, I latched onto a young man I found attractive. We went to a flop house one day looking for drugs. I looked around at the squalor the squatters were living in. How could they live like this? It looked like it had never been cleaned and someone had ripped all the wires out of the walls. However, after my first hit of meth moments later, I moved in with them, and I didn't leave for a while. I was waitressing at the strip club, so I had plenty of money to support my habit. I lost 60 pounds in two months. I also temporarily lost my mind.

At the time I went to my first 12-step meeting, I was back at my grandparents, with no bedroom to call my own, and pregnant. The meetings were the only place that I felt safe. I finally started to gain some understanding about my addiction. I would go to the meetings and just word vomit while sharing around the tables. After relating to other members, I was desperate to turn my life around, so I cast a magic spell for a new beginning. The universe must have had a sense of humor because it promptly burned my grandma's house down. We lost everything.

In some ways though, it was the best thing that could have happened. I relapsed very briefly and went back to meetings where I got a sponsor and started working the steps for my first time. I made a promise to myself. I decided to dedicate my life to healing myself and others. I vowed to be there for my daughter when she was born.

I completed my court ordered probation and monitoring. Then, around eight months into my recovery, after giving birth to my daughter and getting custody of my younger sister, I tried to go to my mom's apartment to take her some groceries. My mom was still using. Her apartment was a mess with squatters coming and going. The scene was permeated with utter despair. Yet, I remember feeling jealous of her — that she could live like this "without a care." I had a brief relapse a couple days later. The vivid image of my mother in those deplorable conditions was a wound that I could not hold space for.

I recommitted to healing. I had finally realized I wanted out of the self-destructive cycle of addiction. I sought help from a therapist. I went back to the 12-step meetings. I reconnected with my sponsor. Additionally, I began meditating and learning to sit with myself.

I used to say my addiction was preying on me, telling me lies. Had I been more aware, I would have been able to identify that scene for what it really was — misery. I would have been able to understand that I was not seeing clearly. Awareness would have allowed me to better understand reality, to reach out to someone for help, and to be there for myself instead of turning on myself and running from the discomfort. Awareness could have saved me from shooting that painful second arrow.

Soon, I would gain new awareness and understanding through the addition of Recovery Dharma to my program. During the COVID-19 pandemic, I started attending RD meetings online. I found this sangha in Birmingham, Alabama that was hosting multiple meetings a week. I quickly became a regular and beloved member of the sangha even though I lived thousands of miles away. I cultivated a network of wise friends who I could check in with and talk to when I felt emotionally distressed. The RD program made me a more self-compassionate person as well as a more mindful mother and friend. Meditation really changed my life for the better. I find it interesting whenever I see where my mind has gone. Sometimes I laugh at myself. I can focus on the sound of my breath or where I feel the sensation of breath the most. I can label my thoughts as thinking, reminding myself "Oh, this is my critical mind", and letting the thoughts pass naturally like a cloud passing over me through a bright blue sky.

My practice has taught me that — no matter how distressed I become — I can always return to concentrating on my breath. I can take a sacred pause. I can create a safe space for my mind by focusing on my breath. I used to feel mentally agitated and unstable, but now I can soothe my nervous system. I can use wise concentration to choose what to focus on. I do not have to label things "bad" or "good." I do not have to fixate on anything. I can concentrate on my physical sensations and release the stories.

I still honor my truth by gently accepting my feelings and not trying to change them in any way. I also practice not becoming hypnotized by the stories I tell myself. When I experience racing thoughts, I try to remember to pause before acting so I can engage with others more skillfully. I try to engage with myself more skillfully too. I talk to myself kindly, write myself love letters, and listen to affirmations relative to my mood. I try to remember that I am human, and I can accept the ebbs and flows of this experience.

I am intentional with my time now. I wake up early so I can meditate and do my rituals before my daughter wakes up. I love trying new meditations and sampling different spiritual practices. Whenever I do a mindless activity like scrolling on social media, even if for a duration as short as three minutes, I start to feel like a zombie. I can hear my wiser self saying, "Put the phone down." In these instances, I can practice mindfulness by listening to my wiser self and intuition that disconnecting is not serving me.

I still get stressed. I am a single mother and going to school. I have learned to reach out to others when I feel overwhelmed. I consistently confide in my wise friends, my sponsor, and my therapist. I try to get their perspective on a difficult or confusing situation before speaking or acting. Another thing I do is check if I am hungry, angry, lonely, or tired before coming to conclusions. I also use breathwork, ASMR, and binaural beats to calm my nervous system and aid my brain in relaxing. I am a bit of a perfectionist. But, when I find I am being too hard on myself, I remember to breathe and smile at the inner critic when she makes an appearance. The breath creates space in my mind and heart. After calming down, I can ask myself if I am seeing clearly or through filters created in the past (i.e. trauma or learned harmful thinking patterns). I can name the unhelpful additional information as stories and remember that they are contributing to my suffering by adding more confusion.

Today, I feel empowered. I try to be present in every aspect of my life. As a single parent and the legal guardian of my sister, I endeavor to never "check out" and I try to treat my girls with respect and gentleness. I seek out information to understand where they are developmentally so I can have wise understanding of their capacity. I try to remember the basic goodness in people. I recognize that each person is dealing with their own complications, which are causing them to react in habitual ways.

Since I have found Recovery Dharma, I have also been able to help others with their recovery. And I can do this because I now sincerely know that I no longer doubt my own ability to recover. I have become confident that this journey of lifelong growth is the path I was meant to walk. I will continue to dedicate my life to my personal evolution and healing, and I will keep spreading love and light endlessly. My goal is to leave every moment better than I found it. Anything that passes by me will experience my love.

NED

About seven years ago my administrative assistant told me that I had an urgent call from my significant other. I stopped typing on my computer and grabbed the phone. My partner, Victor, did not wait for me to say hello. "There's someone here at the house from the water company telling me he is turning off our water service!" he shouted into the phone. What? I thought for a minute. I owned the house, lived there with Victor for about thirteen years, was a partner in a prestigious law firm, had all the outward appearances of a successful attorney, and yet my $100 water bill that was sixty days overdue. I had Victor put the guy on the phone and begged him to stop and take a credit card for payment. He said all right. I flipped through my wallet looking for a credit card that still had $100 available and took my best guess. It worked. No water shutoff. Lucky me? Not so much.

How did life get to that chaotic point? Well, I was in a ten-year "relapse" after abstaining from gambling. I had been clean for twelve years at one point, then went back out, and stopped and started in spurts and fits…. until I just gambled until I couldn't gamble anymore. In 12-step recovery I always disliked the term "slip," as I believed the central theme of Gambler's Anonymous — the desire to stop gambling — was the most crucial requirement to progress into recovery. I knew I didn't "slip." Rather, over a period of several years of not working any program, I had lost the desire to abstain. Once that desire was gone, I felt no barriers and reentered the gambling arena with a vengeance.

The compulsion took over my life, as I started to spend more time at local casinos than at my law office. I went before work. I went after work. Initially, I brought a limited amount of cash with me sufficient to "play" for a while and left when it was gone. If I won, I might leave with some winnings, but returned within days to gamble away the winnings (and more). Over the period of about five years, I depleted my checking and savings accounts, drew down most of my retirement accounts (for which I still owe taxes on to this day), and worse, had to borrow against my house (which I eventually had to sell to get out of the large mortgage payments), used other people's money (which caused massive shame and self -loathing), and had to borrow from payday lenders against my cars (which were old and needed to be replaced in the first place).

Gamblers learn as I did that it is not just about the lost money. We lose time. We lose focus, perspective, integrity, and drive. Our primary relationships falter. Our family and friends can sense that there is a hidden problem even if they don't become fully aware of the real problem. Our actions poison relationships with family, friends and colleagues. I experienced all these losses. Victor no longer trusted me. I rarely came home until the sun was coming up and he was leaving for his job. I was short-tempered. I was in that mode where one only looks at everything or every person in their life as a means to get something else. For me, that was to get money to gamble and to somehow survive until I could gamble again.

During most of my life, I was active in the LGBTQ and Jewish communities, my legal profession, community service, and in health and education charities. Losing the drive, focus, time, and resources that I used to bring to this work resulted in it all but evaporating from my life. My creative outlets in hobbies such as photography, cooking, writing, and music also dried up. Instead, I spent the majority of my days figuring out the minimum things that I needed to do to just "get by" at work and in life and then spent the rest of the day gambling, figuring out how to get more money to gamble, how to cover the increasing dangers from maxed-out credit cards, NSF checks, and ridiculously high cost payday loans. I had to sell assets or let them go, such as a timeshare which I could no longer pay the yearly maintenance, and some artwork I had managed to collect over the years. I canceled vacations. I canceled home services. Victor picked up the slack around the house but not without just-cause for multiple resentments. In sum, everything I had worked on and for over the years — a stable relationship, a successful workplace, community engagement and a reputation for integrity, were all crumbling under the weight of my insatiable compulsion to gamble.

When I look back at the chaos and suffering during the days in my active addiction, I am most cognizant of my loss of choices. It often felt like my car simply took me to the casino after work. My ability to make wise or safe choices was completely obliterated. The tentacles of my addictive cravings wrapped around every nook and cranny of my brain until I became focused on one thing…gambling, or as its often called, "staying in action."

I somehow had a block against going back to my 12-step program after all those years "in action." I was not wanting to hear judgmental and directive comments, whether well intended or otherwise, from the GA members that I would encounter. Instead I turned to a recommended therapist who specialzed in addiction. Among the helpful advice I received from him was that I try a program that he was aware of that was based on Buddhist principles in lieu of the traditional 12-step approach. I followed his advice and never looked back. At Recovery Dharma, I found a non-judgmental space where I could make changes and have a unique and empowered recovery experience.

Through my time in Buddhist recovery programs, and most actively and consistently in Recovery Dharma, I have learned that I DO have choices. I can choose how I act in the face of stress, disappointment, and even happiness. Developing a meditation practice, attending and chairing meetings, writing detailed inquiries, meeting with sangha members outside meetings to share our experiences — have all been key components in finding a better way to live. Learning the difference between feelings and emotions on one hand, and wise action on the other, changed everything for me. It opened me up to change my conduct and choose the compassionate or loving response to tough situations. Along with seeking forgiveness from those I harmed, learning how to act compassionately and practice forgiveness — of myself and others — are key lessons I have gained from working through the path suggested by RD.

It is not magic. It is not instantaneous. It takes work. For an addict, that is very frustrating. We want things right now. I was in active gambling addiction in the last round for about fifteen years, and yet I expected the cleanup would take a year or two. How many journeys work like that? Experiencing the length of time it is taking for me to dig out much of the mess that I created through my own actions is one of the hardest but most important lessons I have learned. Not letting that ongoing experience follow me like a cloud is also part of the learning. Letting go of "what was" and living in "what is" has been key to improving my life. And so if it takes longer than I hoped to get right again, I have also learned to let go of the idea of instantly getting my old life "back."

A compulsive gambler always thinks about "getting it back." The next bet, the next machine, the next deal, the next hand… always beckon with a mysterious allure of an instant fix. That unreal imagery is not for me anymore.

Today I try to live in the present, in the day, in the meeting, in the concert — in the moment. I make sure that I am mindful of what is happening and how I am experiencing it right at that moment. I double check with myself and sift through emotions and feelings to understand how they inform what might be my most constructive or compassionate reaction. I ask myself what is the wisest response in light of these considerations. The issues do not have to be monumental — they can be as everyday as how I consciously respond to a rude sales clerk to the response I provide to an employee that delivers a disappointing performance on an assigned project. Working through situations with the ability to provide a considered response over a knee-jerk reaction provides a much more satisfying and peaceful way to live.

Certain other key concepts from RD enhance the path forward. Service has been key in my recovery, from starting meetings to helping other members with their projects. Sangha has also been important. The connections we make through service and activity within a sangha create a web of protection based on a couple of important attributes that we rarely experience during active addiction: trust and honesty! We learn that we can have relationships based on these qualities outside of the sangha too. Life does get better. Slow progress is always better than a slide backwards because there is no guarantee that we can overcome the next low.

Finally, the RD program and our recoveries rest on our reaching out when we feel vulnerable. It is not easy for an addict, as we spend so much of our active addiction making sure we don't need anyone else and certainly never showing our vulnerability. I have learned that reaching out for help is a crucial part of the transformation from being lost to following the path. It feels risky, but it's proven less risky for me than a spin of a wheel or the turn of a card. The journey on which I find myself today through RD is one of positive transformation. I hope you start or continue your individual journey and follow your own path toward a better life. The RD program is here for you. Reach out.

KARA

At about age six, I realized I was different than my family and people around me. I often felt like I was in the wrong family because it appeared from their reactions that no one thought or felt like I did. My experience was that I was either too much or not enough. Due to the discomfort that arose from being me, I found my first solace in imagination and day-dreaming. Escaping my reality to a world I imagined was my first "drug of choice." In that world, I was accepted, included, and belonged.

My heart ached to find others like me. My ears perked when I heard about a far-removed cousin or aunt who was in trouble with drugs. I didn't know much about this, but I was intrigued by the hush of whispering, the "danger" that loomed in bits and pieces of stories I heard. I did not have relationships with these extended family members, but I knew in my heart that somehow, I was like them.

The outcasts, the rebels, the creative beings whose emotions and thoughts were so big. I knew that if I could meet them, we would have some unsaid bond. My home was a middle-class Italian-Irish household. My father worked various tech jobs while my mother stayed home to tend to us children. When dad returned home from work, he would have a beer or two. Wine was served at dinner with guests and liquor on special occasions. I detested the smell and had no interest in alcohol or cigarettes, which in the 1980s it seemed everyone smoked and smoked everywhere!

However, at the age of fourteen, the perception of being left out, of not belonging, of criticism for being myself — continued to frustrate me and I often isolated myself further with fantasies in the solace of my room. As a teen, I was confused navigating my social life. Budding friendships blossomed one day, then crashed the next day as I was picked on by my peers. The moodiness and disloyalty amongst peers impacted my feelings of isolation and of feeling different. At home in the solace of my room, I would replay these interactions and rewrite them to be accepted and valued instead of teased or rejected. The ongoing commentary, intrusive thoughts, and self-absorption I felt as I compared myself to my peers was painful.

Then, one ordinary day, I took one of dad's beers and drank it really fast. For the first time, the thoughts stopped. The self-conscious nervousness eased. I continued to drink daily but found that I would black out, so I needed to be careful. I started to hang around with punks, goths, skaters, and metalheads. Like them, I was exploring who I was and what this world was, and experimenting with a plethora of substances. I dropped out of high school. I ran away from home. I was a fixture at the local mall and at nightclubs, which stayed open until 4 a.m. I recall more than one occasion "coming to" with people I had just met, walking in stocking feet in downtown San Jose or in San Francisco as the sun came up.

As for my choice of substances, I didn't ask when you held out your hand with pills, powders, pipes or liquids. I took them all with a smile influenced by Jack Daniels.

At seventeen, I "came to" five months pregnant. I had a few boyfriends within my circle of friends. My self-esteem was nil and the yearning to be accepted led to complicated romances, obscured boundaries, and much heartache. The attachment to being wanted and valued oscillated with thoughts of self-annihilation.

But when I found out I was pregnant, I felt I had a reason to live. Flashes of budding flowers, the ocean, trees in the forest, sunbeams; all the beauty in the natural world came to me. I wanted to show my daughter all these things of wonder. Overnight, I stopped using substances for her. At the time, one could not attend school with a child, so I finished high school via independent studies a year later than my friends.

After enrolling in junior college, I was reintroduced to meditation through yoga, a practice I recalled watching as a child on the show "Lilias Yoga and You" on our little black-and-white television. I was intrigued. I was gifted Thich Nhat Hanh's book, *The Miracle of Mindfulness* and integrated these practices in my daily life. When I was washing dishes, I practiced knowing I was washing dishes. When I was changing the baby's diaper, I practiced knowing I was changing the baby's diaper. Being with my breath during times of stress and times of ease. Being present. I felt as though there was space for everything and there were more instances of ease when "I" was out of the way. The interesting thing is that when I started to read and practice more of the Dharma, it felt like I already knew these practices. It felt like coming home.

I stayed abstinent for a couple years until college. People say you pick up where you left off and that it gets worse. That was my experience. It became much worse. I entered into an abusive relationship, which landed me in the hospital due to physical abuse and neglecting my health. I stayed out of relationships for a bit, then landed in another one that was tumultuous, with more physical and emotional abuse and an abundance of methamphetamine.

All of my "YETs" ("you're eligible too") were happening. All except that I was not incarcerated (my partner was) and I did not die, though I came close numerous times. I was 23 when my boss told me that if I wanted to keep my job, I needed to go to a 12-step meeting. I remember thinking, the audacity of my employer! It was a job at a local art film theater in which all of us worked and used drugs together. In hindsight, this was an intervention. My boss went with me to the meeting, and afterwards we went to the bar and had a beer. Neither of us knew that this was not what one does when trying to get sober from substances. I did not continue attending those meetings. I quit my job and my life spiraled out of control for six months, resulting in an overdose in April 1996. Regret, grief, sorrow, and hopelessness overcame me. I was on the floor when I came to and shortly after, I called my mother. For the first time — or maybe it was the first time that I listened — she told me with tears that she could no longer help me and that I may die from my addiction.

With despair and what felt like having a faint pulse and being near death, I geared up. Literally. It took me eight hours to get ready to go to a noon 12-step meeting, the same one I'd been introduced to by my old boss. Except this time, I announced myself. This time, I listened. This time, I stayed. A couple of weeks in, I started outpatient counseling with an addiction specialist. I worked with him for almost 90 days, then acquired a sponsor, a mentor to work through the 12-steps. I chose this woman because her hair was three different colors, she practiced meditation, and part of her story was hijacking a plane to marry one of the Beatles. I thought, "This woman will not put up with my bullshit and has likely heard it all."

During this time, a few friends and I started a weekly women's recovery group that included Vipassana meditation and mindfulness practices. That group lasted for many years, ebbing and flowing, but the practice was always the same: abstinence, meditation, sharing recovery challenges and strengths, talking about the solution and agreeing to guidelines of wise speech. I didn't know it at the time but it gave me a foundation that was familiar when I later joined Buddhist recovery communities.

I married someone also in recovery and we did service work together, creating a robust and vibrant community. We had a son and bought a house. I continued to hold the women's groups. I've often heard that when we become abstinent and practice mindfulness in as many moments as we can, we will feel better. "Better" does not mean "happy." Better means to feel, with the opportunity to "know" all the sensations of that moment: happy, sad, worried, irritated, loss, joy — all of it!

One lesson for me came in 2008, a difficult year because three people closest to me died, I lost my house, and my daughter went through a traumatic event. One of those who died was my husband, who was killed by someone driving under the influence of alcohol. I found myself parenting on my own again with an eighteen-year-old and a three-year-old. It was overwhelming that one day life is like this and the next, it is like that. And yet this is one of the greatest teachings, *anicca*, that nothing stays the same and everything changes. All is impermanent. That is not to say I did not grieve or ponder late into the night, questioning who I was. My meditation practice and the support of people in a recovery community who mentored me throughout the first decade of abstinence instilled a confidence or faith in myself. I was in pain, but I did not once think about using a substance to alleviate it. Cravings did not remove me from reality, but helped me to immerse myself in my breath, in the sensations, in the grief in order to understand it. I could only do this because I knew it too would pass because it too was impermanent.

This way of relating to myself allowed me to show up in the world with perseverance, compassion, and courage — utilizing every experience as an opportunity to connect with myself and others and share in the depth of what it means to be human. I was asked to speak at recovery meetings about my experience. I spoke at DUI classes, telling my story to folks stuck in the cycle of alcoholism and driving while intoxicated. I wanted to both educate people about the effects of alcoholism as well as support myself in processing the loss.

When my son was old enough for me to leave him with a sitter, I started attending meditation retreats. This allowed my nervous system to settle, for the internal chatter to settle, and to meet what bubbles up underneath, which is often what I distract myself from feeling. I soon moved closer to the ocean and took refuge in a local Buddhist meditation center, eventually becoming a community Dharma teacher at Insight Santa Cruz.

My focus was on the heart practices (*brahmaviharas*), the intersection of the Eightfold Path and recovery, and the foundations of mindfulness. In 2013, a friend shared the manuscript of his upcoming book about Buddhist recovery. The components of this program were exactly what I was practicing. It was amazing to create a local, then global, community that integrated meditation and mindfulness practices with abstinence and wise action to be free of entanglements of the mind while building a life within community.

For five years, I was very active in that community. I managed retreats, co-hosted conferences, and engaged in the daily work of fostering a refuge for suffering folks who were clinging to greed, hatred, and delusion in order to eradicate it. Being part of this eclectic sangha was thrilling. Here were the punks, goths, skaters, and metalheads, practicing while listening to great music, the music we grew up on. However, as with all things, there is always the Three Marks of Existence: *dukkha* (suffering), *anicca* (impermanence), and *anatta* (not-self). This Buddhist recovery community was heavily influenced by unhealthy masculinity and inequities among leaders. Great heartache ensued as people were harmed and a sangha was fractured.

In 2019, another Buddhist recovery program and community was created. Recovery Dharma emphasizes trauma-informed approaches and an egalitarian leadership within a diverse community. I moved my effort and energy into this new community as it aligned with the practices of not harming others, taking only what is offered, respecting relationships, being truthful, and practicing abstinence (in short, the Five Precepts) in a way that invited transparency and collaboration among members of the sangha.

It is beautiful that there are many approaches, many paths, all pointing to the same "destination" — to be free from the Three Poisons of greed, hatred, and delusion. To be free of that which entangles the mind and obscures the heart. To be free from suffering and the causes of suffering.

Recovery is a process. It is not an event, but a journey. Along the way we will meet many people. Some will activate unpleasant feelings, but these are our greatest teachers! Some will evoke pleasant feelings where we become attached — these too are our teachers! This ongoing practice teaches us to lean in, be curious, make an effort to understand, and let go.

I am no longer pushing away experiences with myself or others, and I'm not clinging to experiences. I am somewhere in the middle. I'm not attached but aware and engaged. It is a daily, moment-to-moment practice, walking the middle path. It is in this practice that I befriended my own heart and made space for yours. It is in the Dharma that I continue to uncover, discover, and recover my true nature. I will share what was told to me by many others I met along this path: don't take my word for it, see for yourself.

UNITY
Content Warning: Childhood sex abuse

"There are basically two types of sex addicts. The first type is an internet user in recovery. The second type is an internet user." –Anonymous

"Sex addict" carries baggage that wasn't all true for me. I didn't even realize, "I'm a sex addict," because my addiction seldom involved having sex. My acting out had more to do with pixels on screens and lusting for the height of self-pleasure. I use the term "lust" because it also includes my zombie mind-state — my insatiable hungry ghost.

My primary addiction is lust. By age five, I was subjected to childhood sexual abuse (CSA). I was told it was a game. At the peak of it, it was the best feeling in the world. Since I enjoyed this game, I never suspected this was trauma or abuse — especially not "compared" to others'. But as Dr. Gabor Maté put it, "Trauma is not what happens to you. It's what happens inside you as a result of what happened to you." Inside, I lived a life of shame and secrecy.

I'm pretty sure my hungry ghost was born the moment I realized I could play this game solo and indulge in self-pleasure anytime. *By age six, I was hopelessly addicted.* Not to sex, but to the *neurochemical hit* released by self-pleasure.

My parents would catch me in the act. They were shocked, they would shout, and they would shame me, hoping that it would help me break this habit. They did the best they could with the knowledge they had. But scolding and shaming *never helped*. It just made it harder to get the help I needed.

What I desperately needed was one safe person. Someone non-judgmental, present, and compassionate. I needed someone to ask me, "What happened?"

Instead, I was saddled with a deep-seated sense of shame as my core identity. Despite how painful my shame was, I could not stop. To protect myself from the pain of shame, I developed a patchwork of unwholesome habits.

To cover up the humiliating behaviors that I felt powerless to change, I learned to lie. It was less painful to tell a lie than to get caught masturbating.

My addiction also compelled me to keep safe by hiding, isolating, and becoming hypervigilant. In fact — I recall the feeling of excitement when adults were going to leave me home alone. I knew that I was soon going to disconnect from the world and act out again. And while acting out, I cultivated lifelong hypervigilance and a fear of environmental disruptions, which paved a road to generalized anxiety disorder.

As a child with an overwhelmed libido, many things that were probably normal to other kids would drive me *insane*, like seeing people in bathing suits. Walking through the underwear section of a department store. Or seeing models in advertisements. But the worst was just going to school every day. I would always feel attracted to, and in love with, someone in my class — sure it sounds like innocent love in this story, but to live that experience was to be flooded with shameful feelings that I didn't understand.

These were *extremely difficult* events for me. The feelings were overpowering, agonizing, and confusing. I had no elder or mentor to guide me through the darkness.

If I pause for a moment and look back at what happened, I see why a child would naturally develop the traits I had. These were survival skills.

They served to protect me from immense pain rooted in childhood complex trauma. It's clear to see how these traits predispose anyone to addiction when we list out the traits: dishonesty, secrecy, dissociation, disconnection, isolation, hypervigilance, shame.

In youth, I blamed myself for being unable to control my habits. However, it's clearly unfair to blame the five year old sex addict. So I've always wondered — at what point is it justified to blame the addict for being addicted? Can we blame the ten or fifteen year old for the inability to quit?

It was only in recovery from sex addiction, after completing an inventory, that I recounted and reconciled the wreckage in my rear-view mirror. Doing the inner work of self-inquiry and investigation revealed that lust influenced nearly every decision I made. Here's a tiny fraction of harms that I've tried to restore balance with:

I objectified people — I was othering and dehumanizing. When dating, I would use alcohol/drugs/power to coax someone into staying the night. At other times, I would just prefer self-pleasure over actual sex, regardless of how sexually appealing my partner was. In most sexual relations, I found it challenging to reach climax unless I fantasized about porn — even if I hadn't viewed porn for months. When I used porn, I noticed that my tastes progressively became edgier and more shocking in order to achieve arousal.

Just like my drug addiction, I crossed sexual lines I swore I'd never cross. I never thought I would arrange meetups for anonymous sex or compensated companionship. I knew I needed to hit the brakes long ago, but seeking sexual gratification was my life purpose. Without the hungry ghost, could I enjoy life? Who was I before the world got to me?

For about ten years, I drifted in and out of recovery rooms for substance use disorder. Then I turned thirty-nine in the hospital with pancreatitis, from alcohol abuse. Pancreatitis hurts like hell. It felt like I was getting tattooed inside my stomach for ten days straight with zero breaks.

But it was less painful than the unassisted withdrawal from a prior fentanyl addiction that ravaged me. I considered pancreatitis a blessing from the universe and a final call to awakening. I said to myself, "This is where it has to stop. When I turn forty, there's no way in samsara that I can still be running on the same toxic rat wheel of addiction."

That year, I began stopping. I slowly let go of who I thought I was. I stopped letting others define happiness and success for me. I stopped blaming others. I stopped denying reality. In the calmness, I could see how my addictive habits were all interconnected: alcohol, drugs, sex, codependency, technology, all of it. Incidentally, it was the same year that Recovery Dharma was established, so I could work on all addictions at the same time by using Buddhist practices to address the *root cause* of suffering.

For the first time after some ten years of being in recovery, I finally took my recovery program *seriously*. I asked myself, "How much time was I willing to put into my addictive behaviors? And how much time am I willing to put into my recovery?" An honest, gentle voice from deep within suggested wisely, "Chase your recovery like you chased your addictions."

So when they told me to get into service, I signed up and showed up. When they said to sit daily, I sat daily. When they said to go to meetings as often as possible, it made sense to go to the same number of meetings daily as the number of times I used to act out each day. And when they stressed the importance of sangha and inquiries, I did my best to create real connections within my sanghas and inquiry circles.

Each ingredient of the practice made an important difference.

I used to only share when I thought it would get people to approve of me. Then, one day at an in-person meeting, I decided to close my eyes, relax, and just listen. I stopped thinking about what I was going to share. Instead of hearing ways my story was different from the person sharing, I listened for all the ways that we *shared common roots*. Instead of grasping for external approval, I could finally hear how *authenticity* and *weakness* were the truer currency in rooms of recovery.

I made a hard but wise choice, regarding renunciation from love and lust. I decided that, based on my past, *I was unsafe to myself* if I pursued recovery friendships with those whom I felt attracted to. Some of y'all might be able to handle that, but for this love and lust addict, I might as well be playing Russian roulette with my recovery. It was easier to fully renounce attractive recovery friends for the time, than to eventually have both my recovery and my heart shattered. I learned to love the new life of having *true intimacy* with friends without attachments of lust. It was a beautiful new road to nurture healthy relationships.

Additionally, since I had experiential success in medication assisted treatment (MAT) for tapering off of opiates and nicotine, I asked health professionals about MAT for calming hypersensitivity to sexual triggers. "If this aphrodisiac exists, then that anti-aphrodisiac exists," I imagined the Buddha fantastically telling Ananda. Eventually, I was recommended herbal supplements. I don't know if they really worked or if it was just the placebo effect, but I didn't care — within a couple months, I had a breakthrough.

I went on a vacation where there was the ocean, beaches, and lots of human beings in bathing suits. Since childhood, this environment was a trigger where I would obsess uncontrollably about the beautiful people passing by. But on that vacation, I was different. People were still beautiful, but I observed myself and became fully present to an unfamiliar "quiet." I could hear myself think! I didn't have to be hyper focused on where each beautiful person was — *I found I had a choice over what I concentrated on*. I didn't have to obey the hungry ghost. This newfound glimpse of control over my libido astounded me. I had never experienced this level of equanimity and serenity. I was forty years old. That was a very emotional day for me.

Recovery Dharma gave me a way to own my entire story that was drastically different from what I experienced in traditional 12-step spaces. I used to be asked to avoid discussing "unrelated" addictions such as alcohol, drugs, or sex, depending on what kind of meeting I was attending. In RD, I could talk about all the issues of my recovery without being censored. This allowed me to share how critical it is to connect the dots between (1) my process addiction; (2) my substance addiction; and (3) my complex trauma from childhood. In the Dharma, there's no such thing as an "outside issue" to my recovery when all things are interdependent.

Something tells me that Recovery Dharma will withstand the test of time. Not only because it's founded on a healing program that's been helping people for thousands of years, but also because Recovery Dharma is future-proofed: our fellowship doesn't have to spawn a new fellowship for each new process addiction that arises. Among the most powerful aspects of RD is that *we are empowered to easily create a new affinity group* (special-interest or topic meeting), so we can find others who face, or have overcome, similar struggles. For example, when some of us noticed there wasn't a meeting for people suffering from love and lust, we created a sangha and meetings for it. And you can do the same with your own affinity group. Even though all addictions are welcome at all meetings, I've experienced a deepened *connection, wisdom,* and *healing* with others concentrating on the same topic.

I used to make unthinking comments about other process addictions, especially if I didn't relate to the addiction. Eventually, I could see how I was shaming, minimizing, and gossiping about another person's recovery journey. I was unskillfully *hindering* their healing. I was doing exactly what others had done when shame, stigma, and embarrassment kept me in my spiral of silence for thirty-five years. I've retrained myself to notice before I judge, criticize, or invalidate anyone's struggle. Instead, I reflect on the courage it takes for someone to open up about their inner battlefield. I believe as long as we can honor one another's struggles, this fellowship will thrive.

When I think about the baggage that comes with "sex addict," sometimes my trauma sends me backward and wondering, "Is it really okay to share about sex addiction here in Recovery Dharma?" And then I'm reminded that *sex addiction is the very first process addiction that our book specifies* — and it's mentioned repeatedly. The authors knew what they were doing. Heck, the Buddha devoted a whole precept to suffering less from our sexual conduct. So if sex addiction is causing you suffering, but you're waiting for permission to share and heal about it, our program and our book have already given us permission.

So, once more with love: it's okay to talk about sex addiction in Recovery Dharma.

RANDALL

I was the "golden child." The one who could seemingly do no wrong. Or at least that was the image that I tried to cultivate. Because when I was less than the best, the consequences at home could be severe. So I stopped asking for help, and I started hiding the parts of me that were deemed weak. I put on a mask of perfection, and the weight of it would almost kill me.

When I was fifteen, I discovered how to use drugs to disconnect from my painful reality. For the next 20 plus years, I would become a mad scientist of sorts seeking to numb my suffering through substances. Feelings were deemed unhelpful and had to go. Productivity was prioritized as I had come to believe that my worth was determined only by how much I could accomplish.

I had to be "golden." So I became an exceptionally high achiever. But I was also just exceptionally high all of the time.

Alcohol was first. It was like a magic elixir that made being around people less scary. Marijuana was next. It could numb the pain of never feeling good enough. Finally, after I became a lawyer, I met my beloved amphetamines. They were the rocket fuel that could propel me to work insane hours, so I could acquire all of the things that would finally make me feel like I was worthy.

The problem was — even after I became the big success that I was groomed to be and procured all of the material things that I had been taught would make me whole — I felt utterly wretched and spiritually empty. I told no one what was going on. I stayed hidden because I thought they would reject me if they knew the "real" me. And, of course, I didn't want them to make me stop.

Instead of looking inward, I blamed all the external things in my life. I tried changing jobs, but I still lacked purpose. And I was still a drug addict. Wherever I went, there I was.

In April 2017, I was coaching my daughter's youth soccer game, and my toes started tingling. "Better not tell anyone," I thought, "they might realize I have a drug problem." But 72 hours later, I had a much bigger problem. The tingling spread to my entire body, and I became paralyzed from head to toe due to a rare auto-immune disease called Guillain-Barre Syndrome.

I was locked in my body and in a state of total isolation for about 40 days. I was on a ventilator and feeding tube and unable to communicate with anyone. I was completely aware of what was happening but cut off from the rest of the world. I started experiencing psychosis, and the traumas of my past and my fears for the future manifested as hallucinations and delusions.

I was also going through withdrawals. I was in the realm of the hungry ghosts. I spent most days sincerely wishing I would die.

Those forty days changed my life. I experienced unimaginable physical, psychological, and emotional pain. It then took several months for me to be able to walk, talk, and take care of myself again. I promised myself that I would make the most of my second chance. And, if my life had been a Hollywood movie, I would have learned my lesson. I would have quit for good.

But that is not the way it works.

Nothing outside of me was going to save me from what was happening internally. Deep within me, there was a demon of sorts, and it manifested as an impulsive and compulsive desire to avoid suffering via self-medicating. I started using again. My wife threatened to leave me and take our three beautiful ginger-haired girls if I did not get help. So, I finally went to treatment.

At the rehab, they would load us on the druggie buggy and haul us off to a 12-step meeting every night. I learned a few helpful things, but the program did not resonate with me. I saw a lot of people who were clean. But, they appeared to still be suffering greatly. I did not want to just stay sober. I wanted to cultivate a life I did not want to escape from. I didn't want to feel powerless.

I wanted to be empowered.

One day, my counselor asked me if I wanted to meet with a Buddhist chaplain. "I don't know anything about Buddhism," I thought, "but I'm bored, so why not?" A friendly bald and bearded man appeared at the unit a few hours later. That afternoon, I told him my life story and he introduced me to Buddhism, focusing mostly on the First Noble Truth: "In life, there is suffering."

"No shit," I thought to myself as I stared out the fifth floor window of the psych hospital.

The Buddhist "religion" he described did not really seem like a religion at all to me. It seemed more like an ethical framework for living. He told me that there were recovery meetings at the Moore Institute in Birmingham (Alabama) that used Buddhist-inspired principles and practices. A few nights later, we were allowed to go to one. I walked in the room that night and people were smiling.

They seemed to be at ease. The meditation started. I had only meditated once before in my life, and it had not gone well. I was a speed freak after all. But something different happened this time. By the end of the sit, I felt this lightness in my chest. I could not figure out what it was at first, but I just allowed myself to be curious about it until I finally identified it. It was self-compassion. And it felt amazing.

Like I was finally coming home and resting after an arduous journey.

Upon leaving rehab, I immersed myself in the program. Soon, I was one of the regulars. I noticed that the people who served the most seemed to be the most at ease, so I started serving too. When COVID came, I started facilitating multiple meetings a week to stay connected. I began to realize that nothing could help me more than helping other people.

So I just kept showing up and serving in positions with more and more responsibility. Eventually, I was elected President of the Board of the global nonprofit and found purpose in protecting and promoting the program. I also kept helping my local sangha grow, and I still go to multiple meetings a week. Because that is where my wise friends are. That is where we heal together.

The reality of my recovery was not a fairy tale where I lived "happily ever after." When my addiction shifted to processes such as bulimia and overexercising, I leaned into my program to establish wise boundaries and stop harming myself. Slowly, I started to make wiser choices and live with more balance. My goal was not to be "golden" or even "happy" anymore.

It was just to be present, live with purpose, and suffer less.

Recovery Dharma helped me tap into my Buddha nature. It armed me with an understanding of karma and taught me to plant seeds of self-compassion instead of self-destruction. Through meditation, I increased my ability to sit with emotional distress and cultivate positive mental states. Through inquiry work, I investigated the causes of my suffering and explored solutions.

I used to wake up in despair and need substances to get out of bed and face reality. Now, I wake up early and meditate. I set intentions to follow the precepts and trust the process. I try to practice radical acceptance of myself, others, and reality. When I crave things to be different, I remember the truth of impermanence. When I'm in trouble, I ask for help from my wise friends.

Thanks to Recovery Dharma, I am also a more empathetic partner and gentle father. My family no longer has to be the collateral damage of my implosive cycle. I practice wise speech with my wife and no longer hide my wounded parts. I teach my daughters about meditation and mindfulness, and I can already see how they are coping with stress at school in healthier ways.

I am not "better" though. Just better at being broken. My demons still appear to me on a daily basis. But, when they do, I greet them with a smile and invite them to tea. I sit with them and ask them "what's really going on?" And usually they answer "I don't want to feel this way." So I put my arm around them. And then I have the feelings because - if I don't - they will have me.

I don't have to do anything to "fix" them. I can just let them be.

I also recognize that I am going to frequently fail. That's what humans do. So when I fall short, I try to be easy and gentle with myself. Because I am worthy of love and compassion. This is the truth Recovery Dharma has taught me. And the beautiful thing is, you don't even have to believe that it's true. You just have to believe you have the potential to change and heal your life.

And you will.

Above all else, I try to stay present. At meetings, I listen attentively and stay with others through their pain. At home, I read books with my daughters and marinate in the sensation of joy. In these moments of pure presence, I sometimes remind myself that I didn't have to do anything to deserve this. Despite all of the addiction and trauma I have endured, I've been golden all along.

LACEY

The week I'm writing this, I celebrated seven years of being on this path and Recovery Dharma has been with me for practically the entire time. My sobriety has been built on the wisdom of the Dharma and the empowerment to decide what my recovery should look like.

I was clinging onto about six months of sobriety when I started going to our Buddhist recovery meetings in New York City. At the time, there were only two meetings in the city and one of them happened to be within walking distance of my apartment in Brooklyn. When I came in, I saw a friendly, low-key, queer space and while I was nervous, I also felt safe. The folks I saw there that first evening would eventually invite me to vegan tacos around the corner and one would become my mentor. I wanted to be like these people and spend time with them.

It always felt like I was ancestrally predestined to be an "alcoholic" and to experience the heavy shame that is its close companion. From an early age I was taught about how one becomes an alcoholic and what an alcoholic looks and behaves like. I also learned that it was an identity you didn't share with others, that you had to keep it a secret. My family tradition of silence had been passed down from likely hundreds of years of addiction inspired by the trauma of shame, poverty, and violence.

Active addiction felt like being buried under layers of heavy blankets. I couldn't move, couldn't really breathe, but was also somewhat comfortable laying there, being flattened. It was a way to make myself smaller and quiet my instincts. I think of that Marianne Williamson quote a lot about how we actually fear our brightness and ability more than we fear our darkness and inadequacy.

I don't remember a ton of details from my twelve years of active addiction. I do know that it was fun in the beginning. I worked in media, and drinking was part of the job description. I was good at drinking a lot and it was good for my career. My lifestyle was buying party dresses I couldn't afford, going to boozy events with bold-faced names, staying out until 4 am and sharing hangovers in the office with the coworkers I had partied with. I did a lot of convincing people to drink with me when they didn't really want to and racking up debt trying to keep up with the hungry ghost inside of me. I also put myself in plenty of dangerous situations but like I said, much of it is pretty blurry. I kept going at full speed, abusing my mind and body, knowing that if I slowed down even slightly I may not be able to get going again.

This kind of lifestyle was the one I thought I was supposed to have and what everyone wants to have (besides the debt, danger, and daily hangovers.) I was purposefully ignoring and shoving down my need for quiet alone time, reflection, and spirituality. Through therapy and late-in-life diagnoses, I know now that my neurodiverse brain is easily overstimulated by noise, crowds, and visuals and when that happens, I can become nonverbal. I plowed through all of this with the help of alcohol.

Ultimately this all led to my becoming very isolated with terrible depression and anxiety. I couldn't respond to emails or, God forbid, answer phone calls. I could barely finish my sentences when I spoke. I would trail off and go quiet hoping the other person would pick up the end of the thought for me. I didn't have confidence in anything that came out of my head. I would wake up every morning absolutely hating myself, calling myself dumb and ugly and pathetic. I would review, or try to remember, every stupid thing I had said or done the night before and then reel from the shame. That shame took up a leaden residence in my body.

These intense feelings of low self-worth inspired me to seek relationships with the wrong people. I thought I had to drink in order to find connection but drinking only led me to unhealthy connections that ended up lasting years.

Even though I was surrounded by sober people in my family, I found the idea of quitting drinking to be unimaginable. It felt like, if I could do that, I could achieve anything I wanted in life (I still think this is true.) Besides the physical and psychological dependence, I'd have to take on the identity of the addict or alcoholic. Someone who had to keep this large shameful part of themselves a secret, who could no longer have fun or be "normal". A life of sobriety was a life sentence and a burden.

I made the first steps to getting sober once the alarm bells from my childhood education about alcoholism got too loud for me to ignore. I was drinking earlier and earlier in the day and my depression and anxiety were becoming unmanageable. My entire life had been taken over by the when, where, how, and what to drink. I was scared that I had to hit my proverbial "rock bottom" before I quit but that turned out not to be true.

There were a number of aspects I knew about traditional recovery that I was wary of. I am used to doing things on my own and taking care of myself, so that's how I was going to do recovery too. No "fellowship" for me! I was lucky enough to find an addiction counselor I connected with right off the bat and she was the one who eventually suggested I check out Buddhist recovery so I could at least have some examples of how sober lives were lived. Or at least the kind of sober life *I* wanted to live.

When I first started going to meetings, I had never meditated before so I would sit there and kind of peek out and see what people were doing — are they really "meditating"? I didn't get it. Eventually, though, I figured I might as well give it a shot. One of my late-in-life-diagnoses was obsessive-compulsive disorder (OCD) and when I started out I thought that if I didn't meditate perfectly it wouldn't count. Luckily, that's not true at all — there's practically no wrong way to meditate. Eventually, meditation started doing its magic on me. I found that if I had a craving I could see it and not get swept up in its pull. The craving would be like a hot air balloon floating all by itself in my head and my natural reaction would be to be curious and kind about it. "Ah, I wonder why that appeared." Through an ongoing meditation practice, I now see other cravings, like for sugar and online shopping, pop up as well. I can investigate why it's coming up: Am I bored? Am I avoiding a difficult emotion?

The concept of "fellowship" or being part of a community of sober people, felt pretty lame to me when I first considered entering recovery. I don't think I'm the only addict that doesn't want to be a burden or rely on or trust other people to be there for me (in fact I know that's not the case because we've dedicated a whole section to it in this book, *Isolation and Connection*, pg 43). Making these friendships in the beginning had real middle school lunchroom vibes — except in this case everyone invites you to sit with them.

Before the pandemic, our sangha in New York City would get dinner together in Koreatown every Saturday night after our meeting. Over bowls of vegetarian bibimbap we would discuss our sober dating misadventures, ongoing family dramas, and the basics of how to get through life without numbing yourself. Having someone running alongside you can make you want to keep going and forming these friendships has been one of the greatest gifts of my recovery.

This same sangha persuaded me to enter local service leadership positions and because it felt like such a welcoming space with people truly being their different selves, I felt comfortable enough to join with my unsure voice. The more experience I had in service positions, the more confident my voice grew to the extent that I now engage in full-on debates in our RDG board meetings. As the book says, to engage in wise speech is to use our voice, especially if we've felt like "we don't have permission to use our voices or lack the power to speak and be heard" (pg 28).

Sharing my opinions and thoughts out loud can be nerve-wracking and uncomfortable. Many times afterward I would repeatedly go over — and over— the things I said, reviewing them for their articulateness and impact. But I have discovered through this path that the key to freedom is learning to sit through discomfort. And my mindfulness practice helps me do that — identifying where I feel it in my body and letting it be. Granted, it will be a lifelong practice.

My recovery journey, especially the service I have taken part in at my local sangha and the global nonprofit, has done a lot to heal some of that generational trauma I spoke of earlier. I'm healing myself with methods that are the opposite of what has been traditional in my family. I do my best to be kind and compassionate to myself and take time for self-care and healing. And I enjoy sharing my sober identity and speaking about my experience with addiction very openly. The Dharma has taught me that there is no shame in suffering because it is universal. Addiction is simply a symptom of that suffering.

Recovery Dharma's commitment to empowerment has been the foundation of my recovery. To begin to recover, it turned out that I needed to learn to put my needs first, to build confidence in myself and my ability to sit through cravings, anxiety, and other extreme discomfort. I have been able to do all of that, slowly but surely, through this path. RD has taught me I can trust myself and my instincts and that if I listen, I will heal. The voice of the Buddha nature in me is becoming easier to hear. It's soft but sure and it leads me into doing what another fellowship describes as the "next right thing". You have the same voice inside of you too.

PAUL

I bought a pack of cigarettes as soon as I could after I quit drinking. I told myself I deserved something if I wasn't going to have my nightly bottles of white wine and glasses of Jameson, and everybody knows that folks in recovery are some of the heaviest smokers out there. So I started with Camel regulars, and ended up with American Spirit unfiltered. I went from cups of coffee to extra-large buckets of Dunkin Donuts caramel-swirl-extra-cream-extra-sugar, and from an online flirtation into an affair that almost brought my marriage to an end. I just always kept reaching for something else.

I like to say I was lucky because I started out with a lot of friends who were already in recovery. Noah Levine's book *Dharma Punx* welcomed a lot of misfits like me to Buddhism: a way of approaching this ancient path that didn't seem as bougie and hippie-dippy as I thought so much of American Buddhism was. A bunch of folks from the old Boston hardcore scene — sober and otherwise — started up a Dharma Punx meeting in a recovery center right on Paul Revere's route in Arlington, and I decided I may as well check that out. What I found was not just meditation, but community: people honestly sharing with the confidentiality and safety that, as I'd learn, is the heart and soul of so many recovery groups. That safe space became a refuge that a lot of us had nowhere else in our lives. We built friendships in that room. I met my future wife in that room. And when I finally made a decision to quit, I had people I could call from that room.

Okay, I was lucky. But maybe, just maybe, there was also some part of me that knew deep down that there was something I needed to hear in those meetings.

Fast-forward a few years. In 2013, bombs went off at the finish line of the Boston Marathon, killing three people and wounding hundreds. As the cops frantically chased the bombers through the cities of Boston, Cambridge, Watertown and Somerville, folks were locked down and told to shelter in place. But in Somerville, where I was living, liquor stores were still open. (because this is Mass we're talking about here). I spent that week day-drinking, with my wife out of town and unable to come home. That was the beginning of the end for me; I probably didn't have another sober day in the next six months. The blackouts got longer. I started hiding nips of liquor everywhere. I listened to my sober friends at Dharma Punx share about their drinking and using, and I began to see myself in those stories. To be honest, I think I quit partly because I want-

113

ed to be like my tough and courageous friends…even though my life, as they say, had become unmanageable, I didn't really feel like it. Yet.

I started going to 12-step meetings, which are everywhere in hard-drinking Boston. I'd picked up a lot of horror stories from my Punx friends, though, about the narrow-mindedness and religiosity in the rooms, and so I was looking for something to be wrong even if it wasn't. Buddhist recovery wasn't really a 'thing' yet: Noah and his crew were still working on what would become Refuge Recovery, and books like Vimalasara's *Eight Step Recovery* and Kevin Griffin's *One Breath at a Time* were out there but local meetings hadn't been organized. So 12-step was, pretty much, the only game in town. There were a couple meetings I went to for a while, but I didn't do anything else. I didn't work a program, didn't get a sponsor. I was skeptical — like a lot of people, for good reason — of sponsorship and the Steps, but I just used that critique as a reason to "white-knuckle" my sobriety.

The phenomenon of cross-addiction — of replacing one addiction with another — wasn't talked about much in the rooms of 12-step… or I sure as hell didn't hear it if it was. What I heard was "just don't drink," and I didn't. But I was up to a pack a day, I gained fifty pounds off of Dunks and salted caramel ice cream, and I was flirting compulsively online and in the real world. We'd moved to Vermont the year after I quit, and I found small-town meetings even more grumpy and Jesus-y than my old Cambridge home group. I was in free-fall. I started to think that it wouldn't be a big deal to just taste some of those famous Vermont microbrews and small-batch liquors. And my flirtations became long, graphic, intense conversations that took up hours of my days.

You can probably see where this is going. Eventually, my wife found out.

I got a sponsor and dragged myself back to 12-step, and it helped. It did. I worked the Steps, and I got a shrink and a prescription for Prozac because I felt like home-cooked crap 24 hours a day. My Fourth Step was a long, detailed narrative of all the people I'd screwed over with my drinking, using, and womanizing, and what a waste of skin I'd been for as long as I could remember. My wife hadn't left — yet — but it was still a day-to-day thing. I switched from cigarettes to caramel-flavored nicotine vape, but I was constantly restless, unsettled, and filled with self-rage.

And then, I got lucky. Again.

One day, I was meditating on my back porch using the Insight Timer app and I got a friend request. My new friend gave me some suggestions for guided meditations and told me about a Refuge Recovery meeting they were starting up in our little town. So, almost on a whim, I showed up. I read the book and came back most every week, and that's when things started to shift. I finally had a group of people I could be real with, like the Punx back in Boston. And I started to see how Buddhism and recovery fit together.

But this path brought me face to face, again and again, with what in the Recovery Dharma book we call the "heart practices:" appreciative joy, compassion, lovingkindness, and equanimity. Getting into my heart — getting comfortable with my heart — has been the absolute key to my recovery and, especially at the start, was one of the hardest things I've ever tried to do. I can't even remember how many times I completely shut down right at the start of mettā (lovingkindness) meditation. Why? Because usually the way it begins is that you're supposed to send mettā to yourself. And I would just nope right the hell out of that. To the cynic in me, it just seemed like hippie-dippy nonsense. Deeper down, though? I just could not connect to the feeling of wanting myself to be well. I had this unconscious message in me that I had to be tough on myself if I was going to get anywhere in my recovery. What I didn't realize yet is that it was just the opposite: staying hard and closed was keeping me stuck.

An opening came when a wise friend shared a recorded meditation — I think maybe it was led by Tara Brach, but I'm not sure — that started by sending mettā to a loved one rather than yourself. I didn't have a hard time with that, so I was able to stay with it. The focus of the meditation then moved on to a neutral person, to a difficult person, and to the whole world, and only then asked me to send mettā to myself. This was the break that I needed: the realization that if I could send well-wishes to the worst people in the world — dictators, murderers, people who spoil the ends of movies — I could also send them to me.

This let me make some space in my mind and heart so I could stay present rather than shutting down into judgment, self-hatred, and fear. I stopped needing to numb that suffering with something, anything: nicotine, sugar, social media, whatever. I started to be able to look honestly at my past without getting stuck in a story about what a piece of shit I was, and began to recover.

It made a huge difference to me that in Buddhist recovery we don't talk about it like recovery from illness. Instead, I saw myself as 'recovering' a lost part of myself, what the book refers to as "the part of us that's not traumatized, that's not addicted, that's not ruled by fear or shame" the part, it says, "where wisdom comes from" (pg 2). I became kinder, more patient, and a better wise friend to others because I had started to care about the suffering I'd been causing myself for so long. And instead of giving myself a hard time for giving myself a hard time, I could soften into it. I could see how my suffering was like the suffering of others. And I could finally, authentically, let my heart open.

And again, I do feel like I've been lucky. I'll never deny that. At the same time, I have gratitude for the part of me "where wisdom comes from:" the part that was looking for healing before I even knew that's what I needed. I've come to trust that part of me, and I've been fortunate to be in community with other people who have recovered what the book calls "the pure, radiant, courageous heart where we find our potential for awakening." We've grown together as wise friends and supported each other through hard times and good. I was able to be present enough to heal my marriage through years of patient work with a kick-ass counselor. We even decided to start a family: something I never thought I would be grown-up enough or emotionally stable enough to do. I went back to school, earned a master's degree, and started to teach writing at a local community college. And I've been able to be of service to other people in recovery: facilitating my home group, acting as a mentor, and bringing a Recovery Dharma meeting into an inpatient detox facility.

So whenever anybody asks about it, I try to encourage them to lean in to that hippie-dippy nonsense. It might be easy, or it might be as hard as it's been for me.

But I always say, and I always will, that it is absolutely, without a doubt, 100% worth it.

EUNSUNG
Content Warning: Suicide

I was born in South Korea and grew up in a rural area near the demilitarized zone. Overall, I had a happy childhood, but I also had to endure several episodes of violence and trauma. It is only through the healing of recovery and living a spiritual life that I can look back with joy and have compassion for my family and the generations of people who had to experience the suffering of living in that impoverished and war-torn area.

When I was in the third grade, my family immigrated to the mountains of Appalachia in North Carolina. I already felt different before coming to the United States, but when I arrived I really felt out of place. I experienced what it was like to be othered. Due to the racism prevalent in the area, I felt isolated and unsafe at school and around town.

When I got drunk and high for the first time, none of the heaviness of what I was experiencing mattered anymore. The name-calling and stares from other kids faded away. I felt like I could breathe deeply for the first time. I was painfully shy, and alcohol and drugs gave me the power to connect with others. I never thought substances would take me to a dark place. The tragedy of addiction was that what I thought was a solution to my suffering would eventually create more suffering for myself and my loved ones.

I first found meditation when I was in college and read a neat little book on Taoist Alchemy. I meditated for the first time visualizing a golden egg melting down my body. I still drank and got high, even while meditating. I can see now that I was using meditation as another escape. I wasn't at peace with my present reality. I always ran.

The next few years were a blur. After I graduated college, I worked as a wilderness camp counselor. One day, I had an alcohol-induced "epiphany." I thought, if this is all there is to life, then screw it, I am going to kill myself. But I also thought that I would like to see New Mexico before I died. Instead of driving back to work, I started driving west to Mt. Taylor in New Mexico. I walked out into the woods thinking I would have some grand spiritual experience. I didn't find enlightenment, but I did decide to not give up on life that day.

I didn't get into recovery then. It would take multiple suicide attempts, lots of punk shows, and more aimless wandering before I found my way to healing. I still meditated periodically and I found some peace in Buddhist communities. But I am not sure if my sitting against a wall doing zazen eventually led me to where I am now. I was lost, and it felt like I was always aimlessly pursuing a new relationship or going to a new place to quiet the discomfort I felt on the inside. I lost relationships and career opportunities due to drugs and alcohol. It was a bit of a blur, but during this period I made multiple attempts at taking my life and none of them were successful. I felt so empty. I was lost in dukkha.

I was living with my father and helping out at his church. I thought maybe I could bring anarchist philosophy into Christianity and wake up the boys I taught in bible study. So I went to a prestigious grad school in North Carolina and tried to appear spiritual. I also got involved with the Buddhist community at the school, and I led the morning sits on a regular basis. I was studying theology, interning at churches, leading youth groups, preaching, and leading prayer groups. I felt fake as I lived a double life. I was studying how to be a spiritual leader to others while I was hung over and miserable in my own life. I was not able to practice what I preached. I thought that if people could see how I really felt on the inside and the life I led, they would all reject me. At this time, my physical health started to deteriorate quickly as well.

I left graduate school with a degree and lived and worked at an interfaith community in Washington, D.C. where people with and without intellectual disabilities shared life together. I once again lived a double life. I spent days being with people in a community that taught me to embrace my vulnerability, but at night I would numb my feelings by drinking. In the beginning, I would go out to bars in my neighborhood with friends, but toward the end I preferred drinking alone in my basement. Once again, my addiction led me to self-harm and suicidal thoughts.

It was at that dark moment that I finally admitted to someone that I might have a problem. I finally got into recovery in October 2011. It hasn't been a perfect journey, but I am grateful for each moment and each day. I got clean initially through 12-step programs, but meditation was vital to my recovery. I had to relearn to meditate when I got clean. Sometimes, staring at a lit candle to start my day was the only peace I had from the chaos of my thoughts.

I moved to Virginia in 2014. At the time, I was married and expecting the birth of a daughter. I got connected to the recovery community in a new place and kept meditating and walking the path as best I could. I would sometimes meditate with my daughter sleeping on my chest, feeling her breath against mine. It truly is an amazing gift to be a parent in recovery.

I like to tell people that I found my way to Buddhist recovery by accident. I asked a friend from a 12-step group to start an 11th-step meeting with me, and they declined but instead asked me if I wanted to start a Refuge Recovery meeting. I had never heard of a recovery program that utilized Buddhist principles. In June 2014, we held our first meeting. Ever since then, my sangha has been vital to my recovery. Especially when I went through a divorce, the meetings became a safe place for me to just sit in silence and fall apart.

In 2019, I went to the Refuge Recovery annual conference in Chicago, and it felt like all hell had broken loose. I was in shock going to my first Buddhist recovery conference and walking into division. It turned out that was the pivotal moment Recovery Dharma was born. I remember reading a draft of the Recovery Dharma book on the L train on my way to the airport to head back home. It felt like my heart was connecting with each word. I could feel not just one individual voice speaking to me, but a group of people sharing their experience and practice. A few people from my local sangha attended the conference in Chicago with me, and we brought back our experience and shared why it was so vital that our sangha transition to Recovery Dharma. Shortly after that, all of[the meetings in our area voted to switch from Refuge to RD.

I thought all the turmoil and chaos would be over, but little did I know another storm was coming. My local sangha was based in a city full of Confederate monuments, and it would be the epicenter of protests in the aftermath of George Floyd's murder — in the middle of the COVID-19 pandemic. The monuments fell, and I had my practice to guide me so I could skillfully listen to my conscience without causing more suffering to myself and others. Some of my sangha's members died from overdose or addiction-related health reasons. It was a strange time, and I am still processing all the grief and loss. I decided to start another Recovery Dharma group online, and I facilitated and participated in inquiry circles. I tried to help others and live by the Four Noble Truths and the Eightfold Path.

My life today is one of increased connection and hope. As a hospice chaplain and grief counselor, I use my practice to be present and help others pass through times of transition and loss. I try to touch my own pain and the suffering of others with compassion. I try to see the beauty all around me in the small moments. Whether I am surfing a wave, going for a walk with my daughter, or even just sitting in traffic, I try to stay present. I focus on my breath and recognize that I can mindfully breathe through any change and I can help others to do the same.

In these ways, I continue to help myself and others through my practice. I practice when life gets hard, and I also practice when life gets good. Buddhism and RD have given me a strong foundation, so I am empowered to transform my own life in a skillful way. I have taken on a lot of responsibility in the RD community, and lately my work has been preparing others to be peer leaders and doing so with compassion. I have found new meaning and purpose in Buddhist recovery and a path that helps me be present to life.

I hope my story guides someone who is lost and searching for the three jewels: Buddha, Dharma and Sangha. And remember — you do not have to walk this path alone.

May you be happy. May you be at ease. May you be free from suffering.

III.

APPENDIX

MEDITATION

Meditation involves a combination of mindfulness and concentration. *Mindfulness* is the receptive state of observing the mind and noticing thoughts and sensations; concentration is the active energy of choosing what to focus on, whether it be a gentle returning to the breath or training the mind by repeating phrases or mantras.

The Buddha taught four kinds of meditation: sitting, standing, lying down, or walking. You can use any posture that suits you, but be mindful when you are practicing in a group to try not to move in a way that might distract or disturb others. There are many different practices to explore outside the meeting, including mindfulness meditation, concentration meditation, guided meditation, silent meditation, and moving meditations such as walking, yoga, tai chi, or qi gong.

Meditation can bring up powerful emotions, especially for those in early recovery, with histories of trauma, or with co-occurring mental health issues. Silent sitting meditation may not always be the right practice for everyone. If you find yourself caught up in overwhelming emotions, you can "tap the brakes" during practice in a few ways: by opening your eyes, taking a few deep slow breaths, placing a hand over your heart or belly, focusing attention on a soothing object, or imagining a positive place, person, activity, or memory. Remember to be kind and gentle with yourself. It's important to take care of yourself during meditation.

There are many different traditions in Buddhism that include a variety of meditation styles. Here, we offer a basic template that you may build on with some of the suggested options. Some groups choose other guided meditations that they consider useful and appropriate for their particular meetings. Numerous meditation resources are available online and in Buddhist literature. Meditation is a personal practice, and we encourage you to explore it with a spirit of openness and curiosity. May you find refuge and wisdom in your practice.

BASIC MEDITATION

You can use the script below to lead yourself or others through a meditation. It begins with awareness of breath, which can be a complete practice of its own. There are also optional extensions you can use to practice with: Awareness of Sound, Awareness of Feeling Tone, Awareness of Body Sensations, and Awareness of Processes of the Mind. Read the meditation until you come to the ∞ symbol; then continue with the meditation you selected.

Sit in a comfortable but attentive posture, allowing your back to be straight but not rigid or stiff. Feel your head balanced on your shoulders and allow your face and jaw to relax with your arms and hands resting in a comfortable position.

Be attentive to what's happening within your awareness, right here and right now, without judgment.

As you sit, begin to notice the **sensations of your breath**.

Pay attention for a moment to the way your abdomen moves on each in-breath and out-breath, the movement of air through your nostrils, and the slight motion of your chest and shoulders.

Find the place in your body where the sensation of breathing is most vivid, whether it be your abdomen, chest or shoulders, or the movement of your nostrils as you take in air and release it. See how aware you can be of your whole cycle of breathing, recognizing that each part of the cycle is different.

(pause)

You will notice your attention shifting away from the breath from time to time. It's perfectly normal for thoughts to arise and to wander into fantasies, memories, worries, or things you need to do. When you notice your mind wandering, try to meet it with a spirit of friendliness. You don't need to do anything about it. There is nothing to fix. Try to allow yourself to become curious about what it's like to be breathing right now. You'll find that your attention is naturally drawn back to the physical sensations of the breath as it moves through your body.

Stay alert, relaxed, and above all, compassionate, as you maintain awareness of where the mind goes. Each time you notice the mind getting distracted or wandering — gently shift your awareness back to the sensations of your breath.

(pause)

Notice the tendency to want to control your breathing. Try to allow the quality of your attention to be light and easy — one of simply observing and noticing. You don't need to control the duration, intensity, or pace of your breathing. Just be present.

(pause)

∞

As this meditation comes to an end, recognize that you spent this time aware of your moment-to-moment experience. You are building your capacity for opening the senses to the vividness and aliveness of the present moment, and to recognize without judgment how your experience changes.

Then, when you're ready, allow your eyes to open and your attention to gently return to your surroundings.

AWARENESS OF SOUND

∞ You may notice **sounds** that come from inside or outside the space you're in, such as sounds of traffic or the movement of others in the room. If your attention is drawn to the sound, just be aware of it. Stay with it long enough to notice its vibration, tone, volume or intensity, being aware of the mind's urge to label it as traffic, voices, music, etc. Try to experience the sound without labeling it. Practice recognizing it as your hearing, as merely vibrations in your eardrums.

Once you've noticed the sound, let it go. Bring your attention back to your breath. Let your breath be your anchor of awareness. Each time your awareness goes somewhere else, you can gently come back to breath, without judgment.

AWARENESS OF FEELING TONE

∞ Notice the tendency to **have an opinion** about things — to like your current experience, to not like it, or to feel neutral. This tendency can also be an object of awareness. We can practice just noticing an opinion or feeling we have about how things are right now.

When you notice a sensation you are enjoying, you can silently tell yourself, "So, this is my liking mind," or "Hello, attachment." When you notice the sensation of not liking, you may respond silently, "So that's my critical mind," or "Hello, aversion," or "So this is what it feels like to want things to be different." We can learn how to notice pleasant or unpleasant feelings about things, without judgment and without having to do anything about it.

As you notice that happening, bring your awareness back to the physical sensations of your breath wherever it's most vivid, experiencing the entire cycle of breathing, one breath after another.

AWARENESS OF BODY SENSATIONS

∞ You may notice your attention shifting to **body sensations** — coolness or warmth, the pressure of your seat on the chair or cushion, or achiness, discomfort, or tension. As you become aware of each sensation, notice precisely where it is in your body. Try to notice the fullness of your experience in the moment, the actual physical sensations such as pressure, throbbing, warmth, pulling, or tingling. Notice that it's possible to stay for a moment longer with that pure sensation, without labels or judgment. Can you stay with the experience without reacting to it? Just for this moment, be curious about the sensation. Does it have a texture, weight or other quality? How is it changing?

If there is a strong feeling of physical discomfort that makes it hard to stay focused on your breath, pause before acting on the impulse to move. Bring full awareness to the feeling. Once you're aware of its source and understand your intention to relieve the discomfort, move with full mindfulness.

∞ As you meditate, notice **where your mind goes**, in terms of thoughts that may be pleasant or unpleasant, awareness of perceptions, sensations or sounds, or feelings of peace, sadness, joy, frustration, or anticipation. Notice these raw thoughts and feelings, then return your awareness to sensations of the movement of your breath.

If your mind has drifted off into a thought, fantasy, judgment, worry, or becomes very focused on a sensation or sound, notice in a friendly way what is happening and come back to awareness of your breath. Recognizing the distraction is important as your awareness shifts away from your breath, then comes back to it.

Notice how one thought leads to another, then another. In those moments when you get lost in thought or your awareness goes elsewhere, see if it is possible to notice the moment when that change in your awareness happens, when you recognize that your mind has wandered. This is a moment of mindfulness. You can acknowledge yourself for noticing that your attention has gone somewhere else before bringing it back to your breath in a friendly and non-judgmental way.

METTA (LOVINGKINDNESS) MEDITATION

Find a comfortable but alert position in which to sit. As you allow your eyes to gently close, pay attention to your body and see if there are any minor adjustments that will help you maintain the position for the duration of the meditation. Rest your hands comfortably on your legs or in your lap.

We'll start with a few minutes of concentration practice to help our minds settle and arrive in our present-time experience. Allow your breathing to be natural, seeing where you can feel the breath most naturally in your body. It may be in the stomach or abdomen, where you can feel the rising and falling of your body breathing. It might be in the chest, where you may notice the expansion and contraction as your body inhales and exhales. Perhaps it's at the nostrils, where you can feel a slight tickle as the air comes in and a subtle warmth as the body exhales.

Breathing in, bring a gentle awareness to the breath. Breathing out, be aware of the breath leaving your body.

(pause)

You may notice the mind wandering. This offers us an opportunity to cultivate mindfulness and concentration. Each time we notice the mind wandering, we're strengthening our ability to recognize our present experience. Each time we bring the mind back to the breath, we strengthen our ability to concentrate. Treat it as an opportunity rather than a problem.

(pause)

Now, begin offering mettā (lovingkindness) to yourself. We start with ourselves because without loving ourselves, it is almost impossible to love others.

Breathe gently, and repeat silently to yourself the following phrases, or any other phrases of your choosing that communicate a kind and friendly intention:

"May I be filled with lovingkindness."

"May I be safe from inner and outer dangers."
"May I be well in body, heart, and mind."
"May I be at ease and happy."

Repeat these phrases several times, perhaps picturing yourself receiving them. If that is difficult, it can sometimes be helpful to picture yourself as a child receiving this love. Feelings contrary to lovingkindness, like irritation, anger, or doubt, may come up for you. If this happens, be patient with yourself, allowing whatever arises to be received in a spirit of kindness, and then simply return to the phrases.

(two to three minutes of silence)

Now, bring to mind someone who has benefitted you or been especially kind. This may be a loved one, a friend, a teacher, or a mentor. As this person comes to mind, tune in to your natural desire to see this person happy, free from suffering, and at ease with life. Begin to offer this person the same phrases of lovingkindness and care:

"May you be filled with lovingkindness."
"May you be safe from inner and outer dangers."
"May you be well in body, heart, and mind."
"May you be at ease and happy."

(two to three minutes of silence)

Let this person go, and bring to mind a "neutral" person. This is someone you may see regularly but don't know very well. It may be somebody who works somewhere you go a lot, a co-worker, a person you've seen at recovery meetings, or a neighbor.

Although you don't know this person well, you can recognize that just as you wish to be happy, this person wants to be happy as well. You don't need to know what their happiness looks like. Again, offer this person the phrases of lovingkindness:

"May you be filled with lovingkindness."
"May you be safe from inner and outer dangers."
"May you be well in body, heart, and mind."
"May you be at ease and happy."

(two to three minutes of silence)

Now, letting this neutral person go, think of somebody you find difficult, or toward whom you feel resentment, hurt, or jealousy. You may not want to pick the most difficult person in your life; instead, choose someone who is currently agitating or annoying you.

Again, offer the phrases of lovingkindness, being aware that just as you wish to be happy and free from harm, so do even the most difficult or troublesome people:

"May you be filled with lovingkindness."
"May you be safe from inner and outer dangers."
"May you be well in body, heart, and mind."
"May you be at ease and happy."

(two to three minutes of silence)

Letting this difficult person go, try to expand your well wishes as wide as you can imagine — to your family, your friends, your community, your city, your state, your country, to all living beings on earth. Notice the immense depth of your own heart as you offer these phrases:

"May all beings be filled with lovingkindness."
"May all beings be safe from inner and outer dangers."
"May all beings be well in body, heart, and mind."
"May all beings be at ease and happy."

(two to three minutes of silence)

Now, letting go of all thoughts of others, return your focus to your own body, mind, and heart. Notice any discomfort, tension, or difficulty you are experiencing. Notice if you are experiencing any new lightness, warmth, relaxation, or joy. Then, whenever you are ready, allow your eyes to open and gently return your attention to the space around you.

FORGIVENESS MEDITATION

Find a comfortable but alert position in which to sit. As you allow your eyes to gently close, pay attention to the body and see if there are any minor adjustments that will help you maintain the position for the duration of the meditation. Rest your hands comfortably on your legs or in your lap.

We'll start with a few minutes of concentration practice to help our minds settle and arrive in our present-time experience. Allow your breathing to be natural, seeing where you can feel the breath most naturally in your body. It may be in the stomach or abdomen, where you can feel the rising and falling of your body breathing. It might be in the chest, where you may notice the expansion and contraction as your body inhales and exhales. Perhaps it's at the nostrils, where you can feel a slight tickle as the air comes in and a subtle warmth as your body exhales.

Breathing in, bring a gentle awareness to your breath. Breathing out, be aware of the breath leaving your body.

(pause)

You may notice the mind wandering. This offers us an opportunity to cultivate mindfulness and concentration. Each time we notice the mind wandering, we're strengthening our ability to recognize our present experience. Each time we bring the mind back to the breath, we strengthen our ability to concentrate. Treat it as an opportunity rather than a problem.

(pause)

Now, begin offering forgiveness to yourself. We start with ourselves because it is almost impossible to truly forgive others while we still harbor resentment toward ourselves.

There are many ways that we have hurt and harmed ourselves. We have betrayed or abandoned ourselves many times through thoughts, words, or actions, knowingly or unknowingly.

Feel your own precious body and life, in the present moment.

Let yourself become aware of the ways you may have hurt yourself. Picture them, remember them. Be open to the sorrow you have carried from these experiences and give yourself permission to release these burdens.

Breathing gently, repeat silently to yourself the following phrases:

"I forgive myself for the ways I have hurt myself through action or inaction."
"I know I have acted out of fear, pain, and confusion, and for today, I offer myself forgiveness."
"I forgive myself."

Repeat these phrases, letting whatever feelings arise in your body and mind. Feelings contrary to forgiveness, like irritation, guilt, or anger, may come up for you. If this happens, try to be patient and kind to yourself, allowing whatever arises to be received in a spirit of friendliness and kind affection, and simply return to the phrases.

(three minutes of silence)

There are also many ways that you may have been hurt by others. You may have been abused or abandoned, knowingly or unknowingly, by others' thoughts, words, or actions.

Let yourself picture and remember these hurts. Be open to the sorrow you have carried from the actions of others. Give yourself permission to release this burden of pain — at least for today — by extending forgiveness, when your heart is ready.

Bring to mind a person or people who have hurt you, and then silently repeat the following phrases:

"I now remember the ways you have hurt me, out of your own fear, pain, confusion, and anger."
"I have carried this pain in my heart for too long. At least for today, I offer you forgiveness."
"To all those who have hurt me, I offer my forgiveness."
"I forgive you."
(three minutes of silence)

There are also many ways that we may have hurt others, that have caused them suffering. We may have caused harm, knowingly or unknowingly, out of our own pain, fear, anger, and confusion.

Let yourself remember and visualize the ways you have hurt others. Picture each memory that still burdens your heart. Acknowledge the pain you have caused out of your own fear and confusion. Be open to your own sorrow and regret. Give yourself permission to finally release this burden and to ask for forgiveness.

Offer each person in your mind the following phrase:

"I know I have hurt you through my thoughts, words, or actions, and I ask for your forgiveness."

(three minutes of silence)

Now, letting go of all thoughts of others, return your focus to your own body, mind, and heart. Notice any discomfort, tension, or difficulty you may be feeling. Notice if you are experiencing any new lightness, warmth, relaxation, relief, or joy. Then, whenever you are ready, allow your eyes to open and gently return your attention to the space around you.

EQUANIMITY MEDITATION

Find a comfortable but alert position in which to sit. As you allow your eyes to gently close, pay attention to the body and see if there are any minor adjustments that will help you maintain the position for the duration of the meditation. Rest your hands comfortably on your legs or in your lap.

We'll start with a few minutes of concentration practice to help our minds settle and arrive in our present-time experience. Allow your breathing to be natural, seeing where you can feel the breath most naturally in your body. It may be in the stomach or abdomen, where you can feel the rising and falling of your body breathing. It might be in the chest, where you may notice the expansion and contraction as your body inhales and exhales. Perhaps it's at the nostrils, where you can feel a slight tickle as the air comes in and a subtle warmth as your body exhales.

Breathing in, bring a gentle awareness to your breath. Breathing out, be aware of the breath leaving your body.

(pause)

You may notice the mind wandering. This offers us an opportunity to cultivate mindfulness and concentration. Each time we notice the mind wandering, we're strengthening our ability to recognize our present experience. Each time we bring the mind back to the breath, we strengthen our ability to concentrate. Treat it as an opportunity rather than a problem.

(pause)

In equanimity practice, we're cultivating a mind and heart that stays balanced and at ease with our surroundings. With equanimity, we come to understand that our happiness and suffering are not caused by our experiences and circumstances, but in our responses to them.

We may begin our equanimity practice by repeating the following phrases to ourselves:

"I am responsible for my own actions."

"I am responsible for the energy and attention I give my thoughts, feelings, and experiences."
"May I find a true source of happiness."
"May I find peace exactly where I am."

(two to three minutes of silence)

Now bring to mind someone who has benefitted you or been especially kind to you. This may be a loved one, a friend, a teacher, or a mentor. As this person comes to mind, tune in to your natural desire to see this person happy, free from suffering, and at ease with life.

The practice is to recognize that although we may offer this person compassion, we are not in control of their happiness. Equanimity helps us to let go of the outcome and to focus on our own practice.

Repeat silently to yourself the following phrases:

"Regardless of my wishes for you, your happiness is not in my hands."
"All beings are responsible for the suffering or happiness created by their own actions."
"May you find a true source of happiness."
"May you find peace exactly where you are."

(two to three minutes of silence)

Let this person go from your mind and bring to mind a "neutral" person. This is someone you see, maybe regularly, but don't know very well. It may be somebody who works somewhere you go a lot, a co-worker, a person you've seen at recovery meetings, or a neighbor.

Although you don't know this person well, you can recognize that just as you wish to be happy, this person wants to be happy as well. You don't need to know what their happiness looks like. Again, offer this person the phrases of equanimity, recognizing that you aren't responsible for their happiness.

"Regardless of my wishes for you, your happiness is not in my hands."

"All beings are responsible for the suffering or happiness created by their own actions."
"May you do what needs to be done to find happiness."
"May you find peace exactly where you are."

(two to three minutes of silence)

Now, letting this "neutral" person go, think of somebody you find difficult, or toward whom you feel resentment, hurt, or jealousy. You may not want to pick the most difficult person in your life; instead, choose someone who is currently agitating or annoying you.

Again, offer these phrases of equanimity with the intention of recognizing that they are responsible for their happiness and ease:

"Regardless of my wishes for you, your happiness is not in my hands."
"All beings are responsible for the suffering or happiness created by their own actions."
"May you find a true source of happiness."
"May you find peace exactly where you are."

(two to three minutes of silence)

Now, letting go of all thoughts of others, return your focus to your own body, mind, and heart. Notice any discomfort, tension, or difficulty you may be feeling. Notice if you are experiencing any new lightness, warmth, relaxation, or joy. Notice if you feel any increase in your ability to care without controlling, to accept that each of us is responsible for the consequences of our actions. Then, whenever you are ready, allow your eyes to open and gently return your attention to the space around you.

INQUIRY QUESTIONS

These Inquiry Questions are intended to be a useful tool for supporting our growth and recovery. They can be used as part of a formal process of self-investigation or inventory with a mentor, wise friend, or group; as tools to explore a specific life situation; as guides for a daily self-inquiry practice; as meeting discussion topics; or any other way you may find helpful on your path of awakening and freedom from addiction and habitual behavior.

INQUIRY OF THE FIRST NOBLE TRUTH:

- Begin by making a list of the behaviors and actions associated with your addiction(s) that you consider harmful. Without exaggerating or minimizing, think about the things you have done that have created additional suffering to yourself and others.

- For each behavior listed, write how you have suffered because of that behavior, and write how others have suffered because of that behavior. List any other costs or negative consequences you can think of, such as finances, health, relationships, sexual relations, or missed opportunities.

- Do you notice any patterns? What are they? What are the ways that you might avoid or reduce suffering for yourself and others if you change these patterns?

- How have your addictive behaviors been a response to trauma and pain? What are some ways you can respond to trauma and pain that nurture healing rather than avoidance?

- If you have experienced trauma from discrimination, what are ways you can experience healing and practice self-care? Consider opportunities to support social justice while allowing yourself to heal and practice compassion for yourself and others.

INQUIRY OF THE SECOND NOBLE TRUTH:

- List situations, circumstances, and feelings that you have used harmful behavior to try to avoid.

- Name the emotions, sensations, and thoughts that come to mind when you abstain. Are there troubling memories, shame, grief, or unmet needs behind the craving? How can you meet these with compassion and patience?

- What things did you give up in your clinging to impermanent and unreliable solutions? For example, did you give up relationships, financial security, health, opportunities, legal standing, or other important things to maintain your addictive behaviors? What made the addiction more important to you than any of these things you gave up?

- Are you clinging to any beliefs that fuel craving and aversion, beliefs that deny the truth of impermanence, or beliefs about how things in life "should" be? What are they?

- If you have experienced discrimation-based trauma or social injustice, how can you meet the experience in a way that honors your true self, without creating more pain and suffering?

INQUIRY OF THE THIRD NOBLE TRUTH:

- What makes it so hard to quit?

- What resources are available to help you abstain and recover?

- List reasons to believe you can recover. Also list your doubts. What might the wise and compassionate part of you — your Buddha nature — say about these doubts?

- Practice "letting go" of something small. Notice that the craving doesn't last and that there's a little sense of relief when you let it pass. That's a little taste of freedom.

INQUIRY OF THE FOURTH NOBLE TRUTH:

- Understanding that recovery and the ending of suffering is possible, what is your path to recovery and ending the suffering of addiction? Be honest about the challenges you might face, and the tools and resources you will use to meet those challenges.

- What behavior can you change to more fully support your recovery?

- What does it mean to you to take refuge in the Buddha, the Dharma, and the Sangha for your recovery?

INQUIRY OF WISE UNDERSTANDING:

- Think of a situation in your life that is causing confusion or unease:

    1. What is the truth of this situation?

    2. Are you seeing clearly, or are you getting lost in judgment, taking things personally in stories you're telling yourself, or repeating past messages you've internalized? How?

    3. Is your vision clouded by greed, hatred, confusion, clinging, attachment, or craving? How?

- In what situations and parts of your life do you have the most difficulty separating wants from needs? Are there areas or relationships where the drive to get what you desire overshadows any other consideration? Has this changed since you began or continue in recovery?

- Are there parts of your life where you are driven to continue unpleasant experiences because you think you "must" or "need to?"

- How is karma — the law of cause and effect — showing up right now? Where in your life are you dealing with the effects or aftermath of action you took in the past, both positive and negative?

INQUIRY OF WISE INTENTION:

- What compassion or forgiveness can you offer when someone's intention is good but their impact is harmful? If it doesn't feel safe or appropriate to offer this directly to the person, how can you bring that forgiveness into your own heart so you don't have the burden of carrying it?

- During your periods of addictive behavior, how did you act in ways that were clinging, uncaring, harsh, cruel, or unforgiving? Toward whom (including yourself) were these feelings directed? How might generosity, compassion, lovingkindness, and forgiveness have changed your behavior?

- What actions have you taken that have harmed others? Have you formed an intention to reconcile with both yourself and the person or people you've harmed (to make amends)? If so, have you found a wise friend or mentor you can go to for guidance and support in the amends process, (which is summarized below)? What support can this person provide as you begin the process of amends?

AMENDS:
- Have you done something intentionally that you now recognize caused harm to another? Who has been harmed by your actions?

- Have you honestly formed the intention not to repeat harmful actions and to learn from the experience in future interactions? Have you begun the process of directly addressing the harmful actions of your past?

- Making amends depends on the circumstance, including your present relationship to the person and the extent to which you can undo the harm caused through direct actions (like correcting a public dishonesty or compensating another for things you have taken that were not freely offered). Ask yourself, "What can I do in the present?"

- Can you address and reconcile with the harm you have caused without forming an attachment to being forgiven? Identify the motivation for making each amends.

- What actions would restore balance in your own feelings and approach to whatever harm you have caused? Can these steps be taken without causing new harm to the person or the relationship?

- If you're experiencing a difficult situation or choice in your life right now, investigate the intention you are bringing to this situation.

  1. Are you being selfish or self-seeking? How?

  2. Are you being driven by aversion (running away from an un pleasant experience) or craving (grasping for pleasure)? How?

  3. How could you bring in a spirit of generosity, compassion, lovingkindness, appreciative joy, and forgiveness to this situation?

  4. How would this situation look different if you brought these factors to mind before reacting or responding?

  5. If you don't want to, can you at least have the intention and willingness to do so?

INQUIRY OF WISE SPEECH:

- Have you caused harm with your speech? How?

- Have you been dishonest or harsh in your communication? When, and in what specific ways?

- Do you use speech now to hurt or control people, to present a false idea or image of yourself or of reality, to demand attention, or to relieve the discomfort of silence? Detail specific instances in which you used speech to mislead, misdirect, or distract.

- Are you careful to avoid causing harm with your speech?

- Do you say things you know are not true, or pretend to know the truth about something when you don't, to appear more knowledgeable or credible than you are? List some examples.

INQUIRY OF WISE ACTION:

- Have you acted in a way that was unskillful or that created suffering? How?

- During those times you were unskillful or created suffering, how would it have changed the outcome if you had acted out of compassion, kindness, generosity, and forgiveness? Would you now have a different emotional or mental response to your past actions if you had acted with these principles in mind?

FIRST PRECEPT:
- Have you caused harm? How? Allow for a broad understanding of harm, including physical, emotional, mental, and karmic harm such as financial, legal, moral, microaggression, or any of the "isms" and phobias such as racism, sexism, ableism, classism, homophobia, transphobia, etc.

- Even if you can't point to specific harms that you have caused, have you acted in a way that purposely avoided being aware of the possibility of harm?

SECOND PRECEPT:
- People "take" in many ways: we take goods or material possessions, we take time and energy, we take care and recognition. With this broad understanding of taking, have you taken what has not been freely given? How? What are specific examples or patterns where this has been true for you?

THIRD PRECEPT:
- Have you behaved irresponsibly, selfishly, or without full consent and awareness (from yourself or partners) in your sexual conduct? How?

- Reviewing your sexual partners or activities, have you been fully aware in each instance of other existing relationships, prior or current mental or emotional conditions of yourself and your partner(s), and your own intentions in becoming sexually involved? How or how not?

- Has your sexual activity, both by yourself and with others, been based on non-harmful intentions? Have you entered into each sexual activity with awareness and understanding? How or how not?

FOURTH PRECEPT:
- Have you been dishonest? How?

- What patterns did your dishonesty take? Did you act or speak dishonestly to deny or misrepresent the truth about your own behavior or status?

- Were there particular situations in which your dishonesty was particularly present (for instance: when dealing with your addictive behaviors, in job or professional settings, among friends, with family)? Investigate the source of the dishonesty in each setting: Was it based on greed, confusion, fear, denial? Why were you lying?

FIFTH PRECEPT:
- Have you used intoxicants or other behaviors that cloud your ability to see clearly?

- What substances and behaviors have you become reliant on to change or cloud your awareness? Has this changed over time? Or, if you have periods of abstinence, were your habitual intoxicants or behaviors replaced by other ways to avoid awareness of your present circumstances and conditions? How?

- List ways you might practice the Five Precepts, compassion, lovingkindness, and generosity in your decision-making.

INQUIRY OF WISE LIVELIHOOD:

- Does your job cause harm? What is the specific nature of that harm?

- How can you do your job more mindfully and with an intention of compassion and non-harm?

- Do you bring an understanding of karma and kindness to your job, or do you compartmentalize it and exclude it from awareness of wise action?

- What part does greed play in the choices you make in your livelihood? Does greed get in the way of awareness or compassion?

- How can you be of service in your community?

- How might you bring a spirit of generosity to your life, both in your profession and outside it?

INQUIRY OF WISE EFFORT:

- What efforts have you made to connect with a wise friend, mentor, or dharma buddy who can help you develop and balance your efforts?

- Think of a situation that is causing you discomfort or unease. What is the nature of the effort you're bringing to the situation? Pay attention to whether it feels balanced and sustainable, or if you're leaning too far in the direction of either inactivity or overexertion?

- Are you dealing with overwhelming desires, aversions, laziness or discouragement, restlessness and worry, or doubt about your own ability to recover? How do these hindrances affect the choices you're making?

- Are you avoiding feelings by checking out and giving up, or through obsessive busyness and perfectionism?

INQUIRY OF WISE MINDFULNESS:

- What are steps you can take to support a regular meditation practice?

- What are steps you can take to practice mindfulness throughout the day by checking in with yourself about how you're feeling, and pausing before reacting to situations?

- What are steps you can take to sit with your discomfort instead of running from it or running toward temporary pleasure?

- What are steps you can take to question the "truths" that your mind tells you, rather than automatically believing them? Identify specific instances where your mind and perceptions "lied" to you about the truth of a situation, and how being aware of that might have changed your reaction and led to a less harmful outcome.

- Think about times when you felt fear, doubt, or hesitation. Now, let yourself become aware of their temporary nature. How might that awareness have led to an outcome that was less harmful?

INQUIRY OF WISE WISE CONCENTRATION:

- How do you get unfocused or distracted in meditation?

- What are steps you can take to refocus your mind without judging your own practice?

- Notice what value or learning you could gain by carefully and kindly noticing where your mind has gone, or what has distracted you.

- What are steps you can take to use concentration to see clearly and act wisely?

- What are steps you can take to be kind and gentle with yourself through this process?

GLOSSARY

According to tradition, the followers of the Buddha memorized his teachings when he died in the fifth century BCE. To preserve them, the teachings were recited aloud and taught to generation after generation of monks and nuns. They were finally written down, centuries later, in the Pāli language.

Many Buddhist ideas are still described in Pāli, or in a very closely related language called Sanskrit, because they are difficult to translate into English. Therefore, the definitions below are only rough approximations, and it may be beneficial to deepen the understanding of the truths behind these words through reflection and personal practice.

Buddha (Pāli and Sanskrit): a personal title, meaning "the awakened one" or "the enlightened one"; most commonly used for Siddhārtha Gautama, the founder of Buddhism.

Dāna (Pāli and Sanskrit): Generosity; charity. Traditionally refers to the giving of alms or donations to monastic or spiritually developed people.

Dharma (Sanskrit; Dhamma in Pāli): the teachings of the Buddha; the nature of reality; phenomena.

Dukkha (Pāli; Duḥkha in Sanskrit): sorrow; stress; unsatisfactoriness; the suffering in life caused by clinging to temporary phenomena as if they were permanent.

Kalyāṇa-mitta (Pāli; Kalyāṇa-mitra in Sanskrit): good friend; wise companion; a teacher or mentor in understanding the Dharma.

Karma (Sanskrit; Kamma in Pāli): action; doing; cause and effect; intentional activity that leads to immediate and future consequence(s).

Karuṇā (Pāli and Sanskrit): compassion; kindness; the desire for harm and suffering to be removed from oneself and others.

Mettā (Pāli; Maitrī in Sanskrit): lovingkindness; benevolence; friendliness; goodwill; an active desire for the well-being and happiness of oneself and others.

Muditā (Pāli and Sanskrit): the sympathetic, appreciative joy in the success and happiness of others.

Saṅgha (Pāli; Sangha or Saṃgha in Sanskrit): traditionally, the communities of Buddhist monks and nuns; followers of the Buddha, whether monastics or laypeople.

Sukha (Pāli and Sanskrit): quiet joy; ease; unhindered flow; the opposite of Dukkha.

Upekkhā (Pāli; Upekṣā in Sanskrit): equanimity; evenness of mind; serenity; unshakeable freedom of mind; a state of inner balance that cannot be upset by gain and loss.

RECOVERY DHARMA MEETING FORMAT

This script is meant to serve as a suggested template. Individual meetings may choose to edit it or use other formats to meet the needs of their sangha. Before the meeting, the facilitator may find volunteers to read the following:

- The Practice
- The Four Noble Truths and Eightfold Path
- The Dedication of Merit

OPENING

Welcome to this meeting of _____. We are gathered to explore a Buddhist-inspired approach to recovery from addiction of all kinds. We are peer-led and do not follow any one leader or teacher, but trust in the wisdom of the Buddha (the potential for our own awakening), the Dharma (the truth, or the teachings), and the Sangha (our community of wise friends on this path). This is a program of empowerment and doesn't ask us to believe in anything other than our own potential to change and heal. We have found a guide for our recovery in the Buddhist teachings of the Four Noble Truths and the Eightfold Path, and we invite you to investigate these practices and principles as tools for your own path of liberation from the suffering of addiction. We understand that this is not the only path to recovery and many may choose to combine these practices with other recovery programs.

Recovery Dharma is founded on, and inspired by, Buddhism that originated in India and later on flourished in other regions of Asia. We express gratitude for the Buddhist heritage that was protected and freely offered by the ancestors of these cultures. For those of us that reside on indigenous lands, we recognize the ancestral grounds and honor those who have committed to the stewardship of this land. We honor and welcome communities of Black, Indigenous, people of color, and all those that may have experienced oppression in gender, sexual orientation, age, and disability status. We dedicate our practice to fostering collective healing and liberation for all.

My name is _____ and I am the facilitator of this meeting. I am not a Buddhist teacher, nor do I have any particular authority in this meeting. I am a member of this community and have volunteered to help lead our meeting and discussion today.

I have asked _____ to read **The Practice**:

THE PRACTICE

Renunciation: We understand addiction to describe the overwhelming craving and compulsive use of substances or behaviors in order to escape present-time reality, either by clinging to pleasure or running from pain. We commit to the intention of abstinence from alcohol and other addictive substances. For those of us recovering from process addictions, particularly those for which complete abstinence is not possible, we also identify and commit to wise boundaries around our harmful behaviors, preferably with the help of a mentor or therapeutic professional.

Meditation: We commit to the intention of developing a daily meditation practice. We use meditation as a tool to investigate our actions, intentions, and reactivity. Meditation is a personal practice, and we commit to finding a balance in this and other healthy practices appropriate to our own journey on the path.

Meetings: We attend recovery meetings whenever possible, in person and/or online, whether it be with Recovery Dharma, other Buddhist communities, or other recovery fellowships. In early recovery, it is recommended to attend a recovery meeting as often as possible. We also commit to becoming active members of the community, offering our own experiences and service wherever possible.

The Path: We commit to deepening and broadening our understanding of the Four Noble Truths and to practicing the Eightfold Path in our daily lives.

Inquiry and Investigation: We explore the Four Noble Truths through writing and sharing in-depth, detailed inquiries. These can be worked with the guidance of a mentor or therapist, in partnership with a trusted friend, or with a group. As we complete our written inquiries, we strive to hold ourselves accountable and take direct responsibility for our actions using wise intentions. This includes making amends for the harm we have caused in our past.

Sangha, Wise Friends, Mentors: We cultivate relationships within a recovery community, to support our own recovery and the recovery of others. After we have completed significant work on our inquiries, established a meditation practice, and achieved renunciation from our addictive behaviors, we can then become mentors to help others on their path to liberation from addiction. Anyone with any period of time of renunciation and practice can be of service to others in their sangha. When mentors are not available, a group of wise friends can act as partners in self-inquiry, and support each other's practice.

Growth: We continue our study of these Buddhist practices through reading, listening to Dharma talks, visiting and becoming members of recovery and spiritual sanghas, and attending meditation or retreats to enhance our understanding, wisdom, and practice. We undertake a lifelong journey of growth and awakening.

I have asked _____ to read the **Four Noble Truths and Eightfold Path:**

FOUR NOBLE TRUTHS AND THE EIGHTFOLD PATH

As people who have struggled with addiction, we are already intimately familiar with the truth of suffering. Even if we have never heard of the Buddha, at some level we already know the foundation of his teachings, which we call the Dharma: that in this life, there is suffering.

The Buddha also taught the way to free ourselves from this suffering. The heart of these teachings is the Four Noble Truths and the corresponding commitments, which are the foundation of our program.

1. There is suffering.
   We commit to understanding the truth of suffering.
2. There is a cause of suffering.
   We commit to understanding that craving leads to suffering.
3. There is an end to suffering.
   We commit to understanding and experiencing that less craving leads to less suffering.
4. There is a path to the end of suffering.
   We commit to cultivating the path.

The Buddha taught that by living ethically, practicing meditation, and developing wisdom and compassion, we can end the suffering that is created by resisting, running from, and misunderstanding reality.

We have found that these practices and principles can end the suffering of addiction.

The Eightfold Path helps us find our way in recovery and consists of the following:

1. Wise Understanding
2. Wise Intention
3. Wise Speech
4. Wise Action
5. Wise Livelihood
6. Wise Effort
7. Wise Mindfulness
8. Wise Concentration

INTRODUCTIONS

In an effort to build community and to get to know each other, we start each meeting by introducing ourselves. There is no need to identify yourself by anything other than your name. You can also let us know the pronouns you use. My name is _____ (and I use the pronoun ___).

MEDITATION

We will now do a guided meditation on _____. Your eyes may be closed or gently open. Meditation is a personal practice, and we encourage you to explore with a spirit of openness and curiosity. Part of what we are doing is learning to sit with discomfort, but meditation can bring up powerful emotions for some of us, and if you find that you need to "tap the brakes" during practice, you can do so in the following ways: by opening the eyes; taking a few deep slow breaths; placing a hand over your heart or belly; focusing attention on a soothing object; imagining a positive place, activity, or memory; or quietly shifting your position. Remember to be kind and gentle with yourself. It's always okay to take care of yourself during meditation. If you need to get up during the meditation, please do so as quietly as possible, and please hold your comments and questions until after meditation.

(Meetings may be either a Literature Discussion, Topic Discussion, or other format.)

LITERATURE DISCUSSION MEETING

We will now take turns reading from the book Recovery Dharma (*or another Buddhist book*), and then open the meeting for discussion.

TOPIC/SPEAKER DISCUSSION MEETING

_____ (speaker) will now speak about _____ (a topic related to recovery and Buddhism, or their experience in addiction and recovery), and then we will open the meeting for discussion.

GROUP SHARING

Please limit your share to 3 minutes (*or whatever you chose*) to ensure that everyone who wants to has a chance to speak. We commit to making this space as safe and welcoming as possible for all members of our community. Please be wise in your speech by trying to use "I" statements and focusing your share on your own experience of addiction, recovery, Buddhist principles and practices, or today's topic. We ask that you avoid commenting on another person's share or offering opinions or advice.

CLOSING

That is all the time we have for sharing. Thank you for being with us today. In order to respect each others' privacy and to create a safe environment for all who attend, please keep everything that was said in this meeting and who was here confidential. We encourage you to continue your meditation practice, your study of Buddhist principles, and to reach out to others in order to build community. Would anyone who is willing to talk with newcomers after the meeting please raise their hand?

ANNOUNCEMENTS

We now pass the basket for dāna, which is a Buddhist term for the practice of generosity. Please give what you can to support the meeting.

(Announcements about clean up, phone/email list, books for sale, free handouts, upcoming retreats, or other news pertaining to the group.)

DEDICATION OF MERIT

(Volunteer may read, or pass out copies to read as a group. Individual meetings and sanghas may choose to write their own dedications of merit.)

We will now close with the dedication of merit:

Refuge does not arise in a particular place, but in the space within the goodness of our hearts. When this space is imbued with wisdom, respect, and love, we call it sangha. We hope that the pain of addiction, trauma, and feeling "apart" actually leads us back toward the heart and that we might understand compassion, wisdom, and change ever more deeply. As we have learned from practice, great pain does not erase goodness, but in fact informs it.

May we make the best use of our practice, and whatever freedom arises from our efforts here today. May this be a cause and condition for less suffering and more safety in our world.

This book is the product of a collaborative effort
by volunteers of our global sangha.
We are grateful to everyone who made it possible: for those
who wrote the first edition, for those who designed, edited
and supplemented new text for the second edition, and for
those who shared their stories.

WHITE 487
YELLOW 591